Saving Sex

Saving Sex

Answers to Teenagers' Questions about Relationships and Sex

Dr Trevor Stammers and Tim Doak

www.DamarisBooks.com

Authentic

MILTON KEYNES ● COLORADO SPRINGS ● HYDERABAD

Authentic Media, 9 Holdom Avenue, Bletchley, Milton Keynes,
Bucks., MK1 1QR
1820 Jet Stream Drive, Colorado Springs, CO 80921, USA
OM Authentic Media, Medchal Road, Jeedimetla Village,
Secunderabad 500 055, A.P., India
www.authenticmedia.co.uk
Authentic Media is a division of IBS-STL U.K., limited by guar-
antee, with its registered office at Kingstown Broadway, Carlisle,
Cumbria CA3 0HA. Registered in England & Wales No.1216232.
Registered charity 270162

British Library Cataloguing in Publication Data
A catalogue record for this book is available from the British Library.

978 -1-904753-14-8

Cover design by fourninezero design.
Typeset by Textype, Cambridge
in Palatino 12/15
Print management by Adare Carwin
Printed in the UK by J. H. Haynes & Co. Ltd., Sparkford

Dedication

To Rachel, Matthew, Laura and Elliot who have
taught me the meaning of enduring love.
Trevor Stammers

To Mum and Dad, thanks for your continual
love and support.
Tim Doak

Contents

Acknowledgements

The questions that appear in the book are based upon those received via the www.icebergsandbabies. org.uk website, a resource provided by Love for Life. Young people throughout the UK and from across the globe sent questions to the site, which were answered by a team of doctors and Love for Life trained youth workers.

The authors would like to acknowledge the significant contribution made by the team within Love for Life and recognize that without them, it would have been impossible to produce this book.

We are grateful for the contributions of Dr Richard Barr, Dr Kerry Graham, Dr Lorraine McDermott, Dr David Rodgers, Dr Valerie Shaw, Dr Philip Shepherd, Dr Bruce Thompson and also Jayne Abraham, Sharon Hamill, Gail Owen, Lynne Strong, Christy Tucker and Janice Barr.

Steve Couch from Damaris has been invaluable with his constructive suggestions and ideas and we are grateful to Liz Williams and the team at Authentic Media for providing us with this opportunity to make our vision a reality.

Foreword

I am delighted to have been asked to contribute to this publication by way of writing the Foreword. As the father of four teenagers, I am constantly being told what I already know, 'It is difficult being a teenager today.' The weight of sexual health promotional messages focus primarily on practising 'safer sex'. Little is said about delaying first sex and being faithful in relationships; the thrust of teenage culture seems to be shouting 'just do it'.

As a General Practitioner and latterly as an educator I have increasingly seen any alternatives to a secular liberal sexual worldview being opposed and openly ridiculed by those who claim to promote tolerance. Many with a Christian or other faith worldview have looked on in sombre disbelief as our gurus of secular humanism have promoted a freedom of sexual expression to young people, while promising to remove the unwanted consequences of sexual actions. Unfortunately, today in Britain and Ireland, there is a high teenage pregnancy rate, spiralling levels of teenage sexually transmitted infections and increasing casual sex. Behind the statistics are individual lives, especially young lives, sacrificed on an altar of ideological freedom of sexual expression, by those in authority who should know better.

The pendulum is, however, beginning to swing. Increasingly, without funding or other government support, alternative approaches that promote abstinence and being faithful are springing up and being welcomed by those who, at a grass-roots level, are working with young people. Young people themselves are beginning to ask for and will soon demand that a more holistic approach is adopted in preference to that which has been promoted for so long. There is real hope.

The vision for Love for Life has always been to make a difference in the lives of individual young people in this generation. Undoubtedly, over the years, the facility on our website for doctors and trained youth workers to respond directly to the real issues that young people face, has been a significant contribution to the realization of that vision. This book written by Trevor and Tim will bring this information to a wider audience.

The heart of Love for Life has always been to offer a compassionate and meaningful Christian contribution to youth issues in the field of relationships and sexual choices. As you read through this book, or scan for an individual, relevant question and answer, I hope you find the information you need to make healthy choices in your own life. Whatever choices you have made already, it is never too late to make a new start. You are a very special and unique individual, loved by God. As you take ownership of your sexual choices and treat yourself and your fellow citizens with the respect deserved, you are creating a better future.

Dr Richard Barr
(CEO, Love for Life)

Introduction

The questions posed in the book are based upon genuine questions received from young people who visited the www.icebergsandbabies.org.uk website over a three-year period, commencing in 2001. The website is used to support the work of Love for Life in delivering Relationships and Sexuality Education presentations to schools throughout Northern Ireland. The programme has now been incorporated into several national schemes in the UK.

After a while, it was noticed that the visitors to the site were often asking questions that had already been asked before. We began to realize that this facility was helping Love for Life to understand the universal issues and pressures facing young people as they move through puberty and into adulthood.

We have compiled this book by using real questions as they were originally sent, removing only personal and identifiable information. We are aware that at some points throughout the book, the advice given might feel slightly repetitive in nature. This is because we have tried to remain as faithful as we can to the original responses and because we acknowledge that many readers will go directly to a particular question and answer that is especially relevant to them, rather than necessarily read through the book from cover to cover.

The questions within the book are from young people aged between 13 and 18. Only if it is of particular relevance to the question, is the sex and age of the questioner noted. The responses to each question are written as if answered by one person, as was the case when the question was originally answered by a doctor or youth worker associated with the Love for Life project.

Although the questions did not necessarily come from those with a Christian faith, they are nevertheless questions to which many young people, whether Christian or not, seek answers. Each chapter is introduced by a short discussion relating the subject of the chapter to biblical principles.

It is the prayer of the authors that you will find this resource useful as you seek to make wise and healthy God-honouring decisions, both now and in the future.

Dr Trevor Stammers and Tim Doak

Chapter 1

All Change?
Puberty and Your Body

Have you noticed that when you are a teenager there seem to be bodies everywhere? In the summertime especially, many of those bodies are on display without too much cover. Christianity is very body-centred. Jesus Christ gave his body to redeem us and his bodily resurrection is central to our faith (1 Corinthians 15:35–57). Our bodies, male and female, are made in God's image (Genesis 1:27) and, as Christians, our bodies are the temples of the Holy Spirit (1 Corinthians 6:19) in which he lives. No wonder that the Bible marvels about our bodies being 'wonderfully made' (Psalm 139:14).

Our bodies may seem more strange than wonderful during puberty, however. Boys discover that limbs seem gangling and clumsy, and that voices veer from high to low and back again in the

1

space of a single sentence. Girls experience the development of strange new curves and a new monthly addition to their hygiene regime. Everyone faces hair sprouting in unfamiliar places, acne erupting like volcanoes and, above all, raging hormones that can seem completely overwhelming. Our bodies can then appear to take on a life of their own.

In the film *How to Make an American Quilt* (1995), Winona Ryder plays Finn, a young girl preparing for her forthcoming wedding by stitching a traditional wedding quilt with the help of her grandmother and other relatives and friends. During this time, however, she meets a 'body' on a visit to the swimming pool and is attracted to him. On the night she has arranged to secretly meet up with him again, one of her grandmother's friends, Anna, shares with Finn her sad story of when she was younger being used sexually and then discarded by a boy.

Finn is unmoved: 'I'm young. I'm supposed to do foolish things.'

'And spend the rest of your life paying for them?'

'Well it's better than spending the rest of my life wondering what I missed.'

'I'd rather wonder than kick myself.'

Finn pauses and then grins, 'I'd rather kick myself.'

This book aims to both help you discover what you may be wondering about missing and to prevent you from having to kick yourself too hard.

The changes of puberty prompt all sorts of wondering about our self-identity and meaning. Am I normal? What will others think of me? How do I relate to them as a sexually aware individual? Understanding our bodies is an essential part of living lives that flourish and help others to flourish too. This first group of questions deals with common worries about body changes which affect us all, whether Christians or not.

Questions and Answers

1. What is the average size of a penis?

Almost all boys worry about the size of their penis but rarely about whether it is too large! In fact there is a lot of variation in penile size right from birth. Once puberty is complete, however, the penile length ranges from 6–10 cm (2–4 in) when soft and 12–19 cm (5–7 in) when erect, irrespective of the size when floppy.

An erect penis is rarely totally straight and curves to either side and/or slightly up or down. Sexual difficulties rarely if ever result from problems with penile size. It is sometimes said that the most important sexual organ is your brain, and there is a lot of truth in that.

If worries persist about penile size, seeing your GP for an examination can be reassuring.

2. I have yellow spot things on my penis and don't know what they are. They are only visible when the skin is stretched or when I have an erection. They sound like genital warts but I haven't had sex so they can't be. I am too embarrassed to get them checked. What could they be?

Concerns about spots on the penis are almost as common as worries about its size. There are two very frequent causes. The skin of the shaft of the penis, especially the underside and the scrotum contains a lot of glands which secrete a waxy whitish material. If these glands become blocked, they can form prominent white spots such that the normal glands can be mistaken for something abnormal.

Secondly, around the base of the glans (bell) of the penis, a ring of small white spots can be present and they often cause unnecessary alarm. These are called penile pearly papules and are normal. They are frequently mistaken for genital warts but if you have not had intercourse or genital contact with another person, they can't be warts.

3. Hi. My question hasn't a lot to do with having sex but to do with my breasts; they are very small compared to other people of my age. I'm in a long-term relationship where sex may happen, but I don't feel comfortable with the size of them. Is there any way I can increase their size without an operation? I have heard people say the pill can increase their size. It never used to bother me but now I find my self-confidence has dropped.
Let's tackle your worries about your breasts first. Breasts can begin to develop as early as 8 or 9 years of age. Though the average age is 11, sometimes breast development does not start until you are 13. They can take anything up to ten or more years to fully develop and the age at which development starts has no bearing on eventual breast size. It is common for one breast to start developing first and fully developed breasts may have a slight difference

in size. Taking the combined contraceptive pill can often increase breast size but this does not always occur.

Around three-quarters of women are dissatisfied with their breast size, most often that they feel their breasts are too small. Real love and enjoyable sex is not dependent on breast size and there is no evidence that women with smaller breasts enjoy sex any less than those with larger breasts. No caring man evaluates a woman just on the basis of breast size.

Though you say that your question hasn't a lot to do with having sex, I think your later comments indicate you realize that it can do. Breasts are a powerful turn-on for most men and once looking at or caressing breasts has begun, full intercourse may be more likely to happen at some point in the future. You say 'sex may happen'. Don't just let sex 'happen' in your relationship. Talk with your boy-friend about whether you really want it to happen and what the possible consequences might be for you and your families, especially if you subsequently break up. You are a very special person and sex is far too precious to give away casually in just any relationship.

4. I just turned 13 a few weeks ago and I do not have permanent nipples yet, but when I'm really cold or something like that they pop out. So is my

body still developing? I have been thinking about getting a Niplette™. Will this help?

Around one in ten women will have either a single or both nipples inverted. This often causes anxiety, though if inversion has always been present it is not harmful. A nipple that has previously stuck out and subsequently becomes inverted should always be checked out medically.

Sometimes nipples do extend during puberty but sometimes not until the changes associated with milk-production during and after pregnancy. Permanent truly inverted nipples are quite uncommon.

A Niplette™ is a tiny suction device which is placed over the nipple to draw it out. They have a high rate of effectiveness but take time to work. I would not recommend its use when you are as young as 13, however, as the likelihood is your nipples will draw out naturally in time, especially as they are already doing so when stimulated by cold temperatures.

5. I am a 14-year-old girl and have not yet started my periods and I'm really getting worried. All the other girls in my class have had theirs. Could there be something wrong with me? I have already had all the other signs of puberty like pubic hair and breasts but no periods. I have been dieting quite a lot recently. Could this be anything to do with it?

You are quite normal. Both girls and boys enter puberty at various ages. Periods normally start by the age of 15½ and tend to follow after breast development within a year or so. Don't worry. Having a later onset of periods can have several advantages including a reduced risk of some cancers when you are older.

Extreme dieting can delay periods or stop them occurring after they have begun. If you have lost a lot of weight you should check out your body mass index (BMI) which is your weight (in kg) divided by the square of your height (in cm^2). If your BMI is less than 18, you should see your GP for advice.

6. Is vaginal discharge normal in puberty? How much should there be and what colour should it be?
There are two main causes of vaginal discharge. There is a mucus discharge which is produced by glands in the vagina and neck of the womb which varies in amount and stickiness depending on where you are in your menstrual cycle. If you are not taking any hormonal contraceptives there will be more mucus in the middle of your cycle around ovulation. It is usually clear, runny and stringy for a few days and you may feel damp at this time.

The other reason for a discharge is infection. There are a few non-sexually transmitted infections which can cause a discharge such as thrush (candidiasis).

An infective discharge will usually itch or smell badly or have some blood with it. If you are in any doubt, though, attending your GP or a genito-urinary (GUM) clinic would be wise.

7. I find myself having erections for what seems like no reason at all, for example kissing my girlfriend or even just sitting down watching TV. Does this mean something is wrong with me?

In teenage years, boys often find that their penis seems to take on a life of its own and things as simple as a bumpy car ride can start off an erection.

However, erections are more usually a result of sexual stimulation. Thinking about the one you love can be enough, so certainly kissing your girlfriend may turn you on, particularly if the kissing is more sexually provocative than a brief kiss on the lips or face.

It is difficult to watch TV for any length of time without some sexual content, even if only in the commercials! If we are trying to channel our sexual drive in ways that will enrich us, rather than lead to harm, it is unhelpful to spend a lot of time looking at TV or focusing on erotic thoughts.

In summary and to reassure you, it is a perfectly normal experience to have erections but it is important that you are in control of what you look at, what you think about and ultimately what you do with your sexual desires and drives.

8. Sometimes it feels as if my sac is empty on one side. Is this normal?

The scrotal sac as well as containing a testis on each side has in its lining a very powerful muscle which, when the testes are cold, pulls them up into a canal in the wall of your abdomen. This is called the cremasteric reflex and is the usual cause of a testis which disappears from time to time. The best time to check that both testes are there is when you are relaxed in a warm place such as a hot bath or shower.

If you have never felt a testis on one or other side, however, this needs to be checked by a doctor as a testis which is not present in the scrotum may never have come down properly from where it started its formation higher in your abdomen. An undescended testis like this has a high risk of turning into cancer in later life, so it is important for this to be investigated by your doctor.

9. I learned from school that there are three little holes down in a girl's private place. I'm really confused about this. Can you help?

In girls, sexual anatomy is not as obvious as in boys, is it? The opening at the back is the anus (the end of the bowel). In front of it is the opening to the vagina. Unless girls have used tampons or have had sex, this opening may have a membrane over it. Inside, at the end of the vagina is the cervix, which is the entrance to the womb (uterus). During intercourse, sperm are deposited in the vagina and move up through the cervix towards the egg cells (ova). In front of the vagina is the opening of the urethra which connects inside to the bladder and through which urine is passed.

10. I am worried about the hair around my penis. My friends always joke about having curly pubes and having so much hair. Is this normal?
Do not worry. There is a tremendous variation in the amount of pubic hair in different individuals and there is really no 'normal' as such. Pubic hair is naturally curlier than scalp hair and it gets thicker as you move through puberty. Pubic hair begins to develop as early as 9 or as late as 15. Hair in the armpits follows a year or so after that.

11. What are wet dreams and should I be concerned about them?
Erections commonly occur during sleep and sometimes ejaculation of semen also happens usually accompanied by erotic dreams that may or may not be remembered on waking. This is a universal feature of male physiology and should not be allowed to cause unnecessary anxiety. Very occasionally, a recurring remembered dream, whether erotic or not in content, may be significant especially

if it relates to stressful circumstances at the time. Such dreams may be worth discussing with a trusted adult.

Chapter 2

Friends and Lovers?
Friendship, Romance and Dating

Friendship is much undervalued in the twenty-first century. There are over a hundred references to friends in the Bible but less than a third of that to lovers. There is a distinction between the two. 'Among all her lovers there is none to comfort her. All her friends have betrayed her' (Lamentations 1:2). Though friendship does not entail physical sexual intimacy, fulfilling sex is based on the same foundations as friendship: trust, respect, listening, caring, joy.

Distinguishing infatuation and plain, self-centred sexual desire from genuine love can be far from easy and often takes time. The defining characteristics of love are listed in the Bible (1 Corinthians 13) both in terms of what love is – patient, kind – and what love is not – envious, boastful, proud, rude, self-seeking or easily angered – and what love doesn't do – keeping a record of wrongs, delighting in evil – and what love does – rejoices in truth, protects, trusts, hopes and perseveres. These traits, of course, are not exclusive to erotic love but neither are they absent from it. If they are not present, then whatever the strength of feelings you may have, you are not experiencing genuine love.

The sexual arousal that results from just a kiss (Song of Songs 1:2) can be so powerful that you can mistake 'being in love with love' for being in love with the one kissed. Sexual intimacy outside of the context of a deepening intimacy on emotional and spiritual levels can be highly damaging.

Letting physical contact flow out of the rest of your relationship together, rather than setting the pace of it, is the primary guiding principle behind the answers to the next group of questions. The biblical refrain that you 'do not arouse or awaken love until it so desires' (Song of Songs 2:7; 3:5) is a wise one to pray and to live by.

Clearly, the biblical perspective, though unpopular in our secular culture, is that sex belongs only within the context of marriage (Hebrews 13:4, 1 Corinthians 7:2).

This does not mean, however, that the unmarried cannot know truly deep and totally fulfilling relationships with their friends. In the film *Dead Man Walking* (1995), Matthew, a prisoner on death row awaiting imminent execution for a brutal double murder, has asked a nun, Sister Helen, to be his spiritual counsellor to prepare him for death. Initially, Matthew seems to enjoy taunting Helen and as she is a nun, her sexuality would appear to be an easy target:

'Don't you want to get married, fall in love, have sex?' he asks.

Sister Helen does not answer immediately.

'You don't want to talk about it?' he presses.

And then she replies, 'I have close friends both men and women. I've never experienced sexual intimacy but there're other ways of being close. Sharing your dreams, your thoughts, your feelings – that's being intimate too.'

This is why, in the Bible, David in his grief over the death of his best friend Jonathan could say, 'Your love for me was wonderful, more wonderful than that of women' (2 Samuel 1:26). This did not mean, as is sometimes suggested, that David and Jonathan shared a sexual relationship but rather that the intensity and quality of the love that characterized their friendship was more wonderful to David in its way than any sexual encounter he'd had with any women. The currency of love in friendship has been so devalued today that most people cannot imagine it without sex. This devalues both friendship and sexual intimacy.

Questions and Answers

1. Hi, I have never been on a date with anyone before. I do have friends of the opposite sex but I get all tense and nervous when I'm with someone I fancy. I end up saying nothing and walking away. Will I always be single?

First of all, don't worry too much about it. What you are experiencing is quite normal. Lots of us have felt like you and have gone on to not only talk to these *scary creatures* but also end up married to them!

Sometimes people can put more pressure on themselves than they need to by thinking that everyone is dating and that everyone finds it easy to talk to the opposite sex. Lots of young people are single and are very happy with this choice. Being single gives you the freedom to spend time with many different friends, focus more on schoolwork or hobbies, and it means that you can travel and do new and exciting things more easily.

Also, there are many people who wait until they are in their late teens or early twenties to date, so there is no need to hurry.

It is important to remember just how important you are. You are very special and absolutely unique exactly the way you are. Remember to be yourself and not pretend or strive to be something you're not just to please someone else.

It's great that you have friends of the opposite sex.

I think that you are in a better position than you might realize. Remember that the best relationships often develop out of good friendships.

2. My parents won't let us be together. Why can't they see we are perfect for each other?
This is a tough one! We all know parents can be a bit difficult to cope with at times but the thing is, as hard as it is to believe, they have been through it all before themselves, so they do actually know what they are talking about, and usually their motivation is their love for you.

At this stage in life, obeying your parents is definitely the best thing to do. Show them that you are mature enough to be in a relationship by keeping the rules they have set down. Although this sounds a bit tiresome, believe me, I know from experience, parents are often right!

Show them that you are good together, by the fact that your friendship is developing even though you only see each other at school or perhaps with a group of mutual friends. This will prove to them better than anything you could say that you are serious about this person and are responsible enough to handle a dating relationship.

Your parents want the best for you and maybe they have a genuine reason to protect you from this relationship. Try talking to them. Pick a time when they are in a good mood and are not too busy, when they have time to talk it through properly. You might be surprised how well it goes.

3. I have been dating the same person for two months now and we still have not had our first kiss. Can you give me advice on what to do or say to get one? Any tips on technique?
First of all, don't panic. Just remember that everyone has been at the first-kiss stage at one time or another and we all know how scary it can be. It's a fact that many young people in secondary school haven't kissed, although you wouldn't think it the way some people talk!

It's great that you have been focusing on other aspects of your relationship rather than the physical side. This will make your relationship stronger in the longer term.

Kissing is something to be enjoyed when you are in a relationship with someone special. Kissing someone who doesn't see how special you are isn't a good idea. You could end up getting really hurt.

Don't get too stressed out about the first kiss. The best thing to do is to try not to think about it too much. Concentrate on having fun together, hold hands and enjoy each other's company.

As for technique, no one can really tell you what makes a good kiss; you will find that it comes naturally. Just remember to relax and enjoy the relationship and take your time.

4. I fancy these two people in school. How do I choose which one to go out with?

Lucky you, it's great having options! However, sometimes options can confuse us and it can be hard to know what to do for the best. Others have been in your situation so you would think someone would have come up with the answer; unfortunately, this is not the case.

Ultimately, you will have to go for one or the other, or neither of them, and that's OK. I guess it all depends on how seriously you take 'going out' relationships but my best advice is that for a boy–girl relationship to be a success you need to like the person as a good friend, respect them, enjoy their company, have a few interests in common, etc.

Perhaps you could get to know each of them as friends first. Talk to them; find out how well you get on with each of them. You might find there's a big difference between fancying someone and being able to actually talk to and get on with them.

Try this first and see how things go; perhaps the decision will become a lot easier than you first thought it would be. And remember, you don't have to go out with either of them.

5. I get jealous very easily when I see my partner spending time with someone else. Is this normal?

The fact you get jealous, I think, means you probably

care a great deal for this person. Jealousy, however, is an emotion that, if you don't deal with it properly, can easily control you and end up destroying your relationship.

A good relationship should be based on friendship, communication, understanding, trust, caring, respect and commitment. It is giving without expecting anything in return; it is being there for a person when they need you, whether things are going well or not so well, whether it suits you or not.

Your jealousy may be a sign of lack of trust and perhaps even a lack of confidence in yourself. Remember, you are unique, with your own special talents and abilities, and most definitely worthy of the opportunity to be respected in this relationship, as is your boyfriend/girlfriend.

Perhaps you need to talk honestly to them about your relationship. Let them know how you feel when you see them talking to someone else.

Remember that freedom to have friends outside of a relationship is very important, and to be controlling is not a good sign that you trust, care and respect the other.

Maybe you just need to hear how much you are thought of and to be reassured that it is you that your partner has a special relationship with and not all these other people. Talk about it – that's the most important thing by far.

6. Hi! I've been in this relationship now for four months and we both really, really like each other. The other night we were kissing at first and then went a bit further than I wanted. We started to touch each other. I'm not really ready for this, what should I do?
First of all, I think that you are very sensible saying that you are not ready. The kind of stuff you are involved in could rapidly move on even further very, very easily and could even lead to sex unintentionally. It is so important to decide on boundaries before you find yourselves in the heat of the moment and unable to make a rational decision. Many people don't plan to go as far as they do, but once things heat up, it is very hard to stop.

Why don't you 'cool things down' a little? Have fun together but don't get involved any further physically. I'd even go back a couple of steps! If you're both meant for each other, you'll prove it by not feeling under pressure or applying pressure on each other but rather you should be able to respect each other and wait.

Wait and see if they like you for who you are. If they truly like you and want to be with you, they will really enjoy your company just like a friend. You will also be able to find out just how much you really like them.

If you do break up, then perhaps it was just the physical side of things they were after. This may be hurtful, but imagine how much more hurtful it would be if you had sex and then broke up.

Talking to the other person about this is key, so you must take the initiative. Make it clear you don't want to go further than kissing and definitely don't want to have sex. Don't be pressurized, and remember to value yourself and your virginity.

7. My relationship has just broken up and I just don't seem to be able to move on. Can you help me?
It must have been very difficult when you broke up. Have you been able to chat to anyone about the situation, perhaps your parents, a close friend or another trusted adult?

Did these people have any concerns about the relationship? Did they see a future in the two of you staying together? What do you think? Could you have made it last long term? Or perhaps it's best that you split now rather than later when you might have got even more hurt.

Could you remain friends with this person so as to keep some contact with them, who you obviously cared a great deal for?

It's hard not to think about all the good things about your ex and how good you were together, even though there may have been many not-so-good things. When we look back, we tend to think about the positives and not the negatives.

Your heart doesn't rule – unlike in the movies. Just accept that you like them. Stop trying to convince yourself that you don't. Don't get annoyed with yourself at how you feel but, more importantly, accept that nothing is going to happen. Allow yourself to remember how great they were and then think, oh well, it's a shame it's not going to work out.

It's important at this time that you realize your own self worth. Realize your importance and value as an individual. Realize your value for who you are and not for who you could be with your ex. Fill your life full with other friends.

I certainly don't claim to have an easy solution to your problem but I hope this is of some help. In time, things will get easier.

8. How soon can you be in love and how can I be sure I really love someone?

Love is a funny thing. It is something we all want. We all want to love and be loved. But knowing for sure we love someone and that they love us can be a bit tricky.

To be 'in love' can involve you thinking about someone all the time, wanting to be with them constantly, getting excited when you meet up and go out, and all those 'bubbly' feelings of excitement and happiness you have for that special person.

Sometimes, though, these initial feelings fade quickly and because of this, it is very important that there is more to the relationship than just feelings. If you find that your relationship is based on trust, respect and a solid friendship, there could be real mileage in the two of you seeing if you could make it work out long term.

Forever-love invests in the other person; it puts the needs of the other person above one's own. Love is friendship, communication, understanding, trust, caring, respect and commitment. Being truly in love is more than just feelings; it's more than physical attraction. It is all of the above and it's commitment.

It is important to remember also that a good relationship in the teenage years doesn't exclude others. It's so important that you continue to keep and make friends outside of your relationship. If you ignore them, and your romance dies, you'll be left with nothing.

It takes time to develop a good friendship. I guess it takes even longer to know you are truly in love and to be sure that this person is the one you want to invest the necessary time and effort with to ensure you are together long term.

9. Is it OK to have sex with someone if you are in love?

Being in love is not a good enough reason in itself to have sex. Are you sure you are in love? Does your partner really love you? They may say they do, but what would it be like if you agreed to have sex and then soon afterwards broke up?

Some young people think that sex will complete their relationship and make it last but more often than not the complete opposite happens and soon afterwards they break up. It is best at a young age to keep sex out of the equation and instead concentrate on getting to know the other person as a friend first and developing the relationship in a way that lets you get to know the person better: their likes, dislikes, hobbies, etc.

Not having sex means you don't have to worry about what would happen if you got pregnant. You don't have to worry about sexually transmitted infections that can cause a lot of harm to your body, both now and in your future. You don't have to worry about the emotional hurt and the feeling that you are being used just for your body.

Your virginity is a special thing and something that you can be very proud of, and remember that once it is lost, it is lost forever.

If you hear the line 'if you really loved me you would . . .' point out that if they really loved you they wouldn't be putting you under any pressure to do something that you didn't want to do. Point out also that it's because you value yourself, virginity and true love that you are making this decision.

Chapter 3

Saving Sex?
Virginity and Abstinence

Few books giving sexual advice to teens will spend long on virginity. It is either seen as something unimportant or even if it may possibly be of value, it's quite impossible to maintain in our sex-saturated world.

Well perhaps not quite impossible. In the film *American Pie* (1999) Kevin, Finch, Chris and Oz are four teenagers who feel that their 'very manhood is at stake', as long as they remain virgins. So they make a pact to have sex with a girl before they leave high school. On the night of the final high school prom, three of the lads succeed in losing their virginity (not all in the way they had planned) but Oz at least seems to be different and remains a virgin. He tells his girlfriend, Heather, of the pact but adds, 'But with you it's not like I'm running towards

27

the goal and looking for the best way to score. I care
about you.' They spend the night in each other's
arms but seemingly do no more. Perhaps real love
does make a difference to how we behave sexually.

More recently, the *American Pie* theme has
reappeared in *The 40-Year-Old Virgin* (2005) in which
Steve Carroll plays Andy Stitzer, the rather nerdish
title role. Three of his male friends, appalled at his
continuing virginity, attempt to rectify the situation,
in the event, to no avail. Andy falls in love and his
virginity is eventually lost on his wedding night
with the woman he marries. Though Andy's
portrayal as a nerd is unflattering, it is Andy's
friends whose lives are complicated and strained by
uncommitted sex with women. Andy's life by
comparison is ultimately better and he ends up with
true love, a wife and, as his friends put it, 'getting
some'.

Virginity is very important for Christians. Christ
himself, though no sexual prude, never married and
was a virgin, despite suggestions to the contrary of
popular fiction such as *The Da Vinci Code* by Dan
Brown (2003, Bantam Press). Jesus also spoke of
those who choose a lifelong state of virginity in
order to give priority to serving God without
distraction (Matthew 19:12). Sex can certainly still be
a major distraction in that regard today and we
should applaud and support rather than ridicule
those who make a deliberate choice to avoid sexual
involvement in their teens and twenties in order to

devote their lives to Christian work which otherwise could not be done.

For those who eventually marry, the expectation of the New Testament is that they should be virgins when they do so (1 Corinthians 7:33–35). Though there is no scripture that specifically states 'no sex outside of marriage' the Greek word *pornea* (translated sexual immorality or fornication) clearly includes sex outside of marriage in its meaning and is forbidden in many parts of the New Testament (1 Corinthians 6:18, Ephesians 5:3–4, Colossians 3:5–6, 1 Thessalonians 4:3–5, Hebrews 12:16, 1 Peter 4:3).

Why this seemingly restrictive teaching? The key reason is that sexual intercourse always has a spiritual component; even what we might consider to be the most casual of sexual encounters, e.g. that between a prostitute and her client, has this element. 'Do you not know that he who unites himself with a prostitute is one with her in body? For it is said, "The two will become one flesh"' (1 Corinthians 6:16). Having sex with someone forms a spiritual bond between you that can never be undone. This is why sex for the first time is a crucial milestone in life. You can never be the same again. Sex is at its best in a loving, committed relationship and if first sex is to be the best sex, it is worth saving it until marriage.

Questions and Answers

1. What is a virgin?

A virgin is somebody who has not yet had sexual intercourse. In my view oral and anal intercourse, as well as vaginal, all involve the loss of virginity. 'Virgin' is sometimes used as a word of abuse but in fact virginity is a precious gift to bring to any sexual relationship because it can only be given once. Loss of virginity in the early teens nearly always leads on to multiple sexual partners by the age of 20, so if you only intend to have one love for life, early sex is not a good way to achieve it.

2. If I have done other stuff but not actually had sex, am I still a virgin?

This is a big question for young people who are perhaps trying to work out for themselves what they feel is appropriate behaviour within dating relationships.

A virgin is most commonly seen as a person who has not yet engaged in vaginal sexual intercourse. In a stricter sense, though, it is somebody who has not yet engaged in any sexual activities such as mutual masturbation (touching your partners genitals), oral or anal sex, or perhaps activities such as simulated sex with clothes still on. Some people feel that being involved in such activities *doesn't* mean that you have lost your virginity. I guess really this question is centred on the whole notion of 'How far is too far?' and to answer it you really need to examine and think about the consequences of this sort of behaviour, whether it be full sex or some of the other mentioned activities which many would regard as 'pre-sexual' activity.

Getting into pre-sexual stuff (further than kissing) can be dangerous, as it can quickly progress much further than planned. In the heat of the moment, it can be very hard to control your own and your partner's actions and sex can easily occur even if it wasn't planned.

It is important to remember that many STIs (sexually transmitted infections) can still be passed on without full penetration, as genital skin-to-skin contact is enough to transmit some infections. There is also a small possibility that pregnancy could occur, as sperm are present in pre-ejaculation fluid and if deposited around the vagina area they may enter the vagina and cause pregnancy.

As discussed, the term virgin can mean different things to different people, ranging from total avoidance of any sexual activity to everything but full sexual inter-course. I feel the more important issue is to think about the consequences of any form of sexual activity and to assess whether they are consequences you are ready to deal with. Do you want to pick up or pass on an STI? Do you want to deal with the birth (or abortion) of a son or daughter? Are you ready to deal with the emotional responsibility and potential emotional hurt that sexual activity inevitably has attached to it?

3. Why should I remain a virgin?

Remaining a virgin is a brilliant choice to make, especially for young people, both for your physical and your emotional well-being. As you make your way through your teens and into your twenties many exciting and beneficial opportunities and challenges will present themselves to you. Making the choice to be a virgin can enable you to face these free from the worry of having to deal with:

- **Pregnancy**
  You can get pregnant: without full penetration, since fertile mucus at the entrance to the vagina will allow sperm to swim up; without ejaculation, since sperm is present in pre-ejaculation fluid; no matter what method of contraception you use, since all of them have failure rates.

- **Sexually Transmitted Infection (STI)**
  You could catch an STI. There are over twenty types of STIs. Some such as chlamydia and gonorrhoea can cause infertility and ectopic pregnancy. Often they do not cause symptoms, so they can be damaging you without you knowing you have them. Infections such as genital warts (caused by the human papillomavirus or HPV) occur on the genitals and elsewhere on the skin of the thighs and pelvis, so can be caught by genital skin contact without penetration.

- **Emotional Hurt**
  You can get hurt when a close relationship ends.
  Imagine how much more hurt you would be if sex
  had been part of the relationship. Very often when
  sex enters into relationships involving young
  people, they are radically altered and may end.
  Why? Because the focus shifts from developing
  a mutual friendship to the purely physical, with
  more time spent concentrating on sex at the
  expense of getting to know each other better as
  friends. This frequently leads to breakdown rather
  than a strengthening of the relationship. It reduces
  respect, how you value yourself, the other person,
  and devalues sex itself.

Remaining a virgin is a very positive and healthy
choice to make. Being a virgin shows that you
respect and value yourself enough to save your
virginity for someone who is worthy of it and who is
worthy of you.

**4. What does losing your virginity mean? What
will happen to my body if I lose my virginity?**
To lose your virginity means to have sexual intercourse for the first time. If you lose your virginity
you can never become a virgin again and therefore it
is something very special to give to another person
who should respect you, love you and be 100 per
cent committed to you for the long term.

In physical terms, girls may bleed a little after having vaginal intercourse for the first time, since a membrane of skin called the hymen (which is part of the vulva) is torn as a result of penetration. However, if tampons have been used previously, the hymen will have already been broken. For males there are no physical changes to the body after having sexual intercourse for the first time. The psychological effects and changes in subsequent behaviour can be marked for both girls and boys.

It is important to note that if someone has lost their virginity they don't have to make the same choice again when faced with a similar situation. They can decide not to have sex from this point on. Even within the same relationship you can decide not to have sex in the future, and this isn't having double standards or being unfair, it is you deciding to choose what is right and healthiest for you. If your partner can't accept this and is putting you under pressure then they aren't worthy of you and you may well be better off without them.

5. I feel left out because all of my friends have had sex and I am still a virgin. What should I do?
I think there are a few things you have to consider. Firstly, is it such a bad thing to feel left out because you have not had sex? I think it is great! Do you want to know why? You may feel left out because everyone else has had sex but it is important to

realize that you are also left out from the risks of pregnancy, developing a sexually transmitted infection and from the emotional hurt often caused when sex enters a teenage relationship, especially if it ends as the vast majority do.

Secondly, are you *sure* all of your friends have had sex? Quite often people say they have had sex and make up great stories about what they get up to at the weekends, just to impress. It is a fact that the majority of young people under 16 have not had sex. So rather than feeling left out you should feel assured and encouraged that you are actually part of the majority who have decided to wait. Also, sex under the age of 16 is illegal in Great Britain; in Northern Ireland the legal age is 17.

It is great that you are still a virgin. Your virginity is a sign that you respect and value yourself enough to wait for someone who deserves you. Wouldn't it be awful if you decided to have sex just because you thought your friends were doing it and then you realized that actually they weren't.

What should you do? Continue to be a virgin and be happy that you have made the correct choice not to have sex because you realize all the benefits associated with this choice. Be proud of your virginity!

6. There's no way I can wait till I'm married to have sex. With all these hormones racing around

**my body, I'll explode if I don't do it soon. How do
you expect young people these days to wait, when
society all around is constantly bombarding us
with images of sex and telling us to just get on
with it and do it?**

This is a very common question and it raises several
very important issues.

Going through your teenage years is certainly
made that bit more interesting by having to cope
with racing hormones making you feel and think in
all sorts of different and apparently uncontrollable
ways. However, it is not the case that you will
explode if you don't have sex. Unlike food and
water, we can survive without having sex. Although
it can be tough at times, taking certain steps can
certainly help you to control your sexual urges.
Being in control of what you think and talk about
helps. Don't spend time reading magazines or
watching TV programmes that dwell too much on
the topic of sex. When you talk to your friends about
these things, make sure you do so in a way that
respects the opposite sex and sex itself.

Waiting till you're married to have sex and
marrying someone who has waited for you, means
that you will not have to worry about performance
comparisons with past partners or catching STIs.
You will be able to experiment and learn about sex
together. It will be a new and exciting thing that will
help to cement your wedding vows and to bring you
closer together as a couple.

You have to evaluate what others say to you, including the media. Think about why the media uses sex – is it to sell you something? Think about the consequences of choosing a certain lifestyle promoted in the media. It is you, after all, who will have to face the consequences of your choices, and things don't always work out in real life as they do on TV.

Remember, hormones certainly make things tough but not impossible. Not to have sex as a teenager and to wait until you are married is certainly possible and indeed very beneficial.

It is important to remember, too, that marriage is not a life of unlimited sex. There will be times when one or other of you is not able or willing to have sex on a specific occasion. No long-term commitment will flourish if you are unwilling to go without sex at times because you feel you *must* have it.

7. I'm in a relationship at the moment but I know that I'm not really in love. I want to wait and lose my virginity in a truly loving relationship but I'm worried I won't have one until I'm older. I certainly don't want to regret my first time. I don't want to be a virgin for too long, so should I perhaps settle for the person I'm going out with now?

I agree that it is best to lose your virginity in a truly loving relationship and I would encourage you to wait for that. Can you imagine how you'd feel if you slept with this person and the relationship ended? You would have lost your virginity to them and they would be out of your life forever. What's the rush? Good relationships take time but they are well worth waiting for. Hopefully, there will be someone you will truly love in the future. Would you want to keep yourself for them? A lot of people I have talked to hope that the person they end up sharing their life with will have kept themselves for their future partner also.

Sex isn't just a physical experience. You give part of yourself away in a sexual relationship. It is an emotional experience too. You want to avoid regretting your first time; perhaps if you have sex just to make sure you haven't missed out on something, you will have regrets. Remember you are also putting yourself at risk of picking up an STI or having to face up to an unplanned pregnancy.

I'd definitely advise you to wait and hold out for that special long-term loving relationship, preferably marriage, that will enable you to fully enjoy sex, free from the worries associated when sex occurs within an uncommitted, shorter-term relationship.

At the end of the day, you will make your own choices and you will create the future through those choices.

8. I'm in a relationship at the moment and we both really love each other. We've talked about having sex and think it would be a good idea but how can we be really sure?

It sounds to me like you have a good relationship in which you can talk about this very important issue. I'm sure you feel a great deal for each other.

If you have such a great relationship, do you really want to jeopardize it by having sex? Often when sex enters into teenage relationships, the relationship soon ends. I can't be absolutely sure why this is, but I know that when a couple in their early to mid-teens start to have sex, other more important aspects of their relationship, like friendship, are often forgotten, because they tend to focus too much just on the physical side.

I know your feelings are really strong and it's perfectly natural to want to have sex, but you have to decide whether it's going to be worth it and what you want for your life, not only now but in the future as well. Think of the possible consequences: you could get pregnant; you could pick up an STI; you could risk jeopardizing a great relationship. How will you feel emotionally if you split up and you've lost your virginity? These are all things you have to think through seriously before you make any decisions.

You may be or think that you are in love, but is that enough? The average person falls in love seven times in their life, though for some it is more like seven times a week! Imagine the consequences if you slept with everyone you fell in love with.

I hope you don't think I'm trying to spoil your fun because the choice is yours and I'm not trying to take that away from you. But I don't want you to have regrets in the future or put your health at risk. Be sure – there's a lot at stake.

9. Is it possible to make your future marriage partner think you are a virgin even if you have actually already had sex?

This is a very interesting question but I am not sure it is the one you should be asking. The most important thing you should be asking yourself is 'How much of my marriage do I want to build on trust and respect rather than on deceit and lies?'

Rather than being concerned with the cosmetics of concealing, you ought to give thought to how strong your relationship is if you cannot bear telling it like it is, or if you fear your present or future partner's reactions to the truth.

In purely physical terms, having sex for the first time for a female may result in a membrane of skin called the hymen being torn if she has never used tampons. For males there are no physical changes to the body after having sexual intercourse for the first time.

Hiding the truth does not sound a good foundation on which to build a life together, and if you can't share your fears with each other, I wonder whether you should be sharing wedding vows either? After all, if you hide your secrets, this person won't be marrying the real you but only a façade of what you want them to see.

Perhaps I have been quite blunt in my answer but I am very concerned for you both and want you to fully consider the potential consequences of being anything other than 100 per cent honest with your partner.

10. What is sexual abstinence?

Sexual abstinence is voluntarily refraining from sexual intercourse and from some other sexual activities. It is sometimes referred to as 'saved sex' to distinguish it from so-called 'safe sex'.

Abstinence in practice is defined in a variety of different ways. It can mean no sexual touching at all, some sexual touching, or everything except penetrative sexual intercourse.

This can be very confusing as you try to make choices for yourself regarding the decision to be abstinent or not. To help you, I have defined what I believe abstinence to be:

> A person who is abstinent does not go any further than kissing while in a dating relationship. They do not get involved in any form of sexual foreplay which may include intimate stroking of their partner's body, touching of the genitals, mutual masturbation, oral sex, vaginal or anal sex.

Saving Sex

By avoiding these activities, the exchange of body fluids (semen, vaginal secretions, or blood) is prevented. This means that pregnancy will not occur and sexually transmitted infections cannot be caught or passed on. It also avoids the emotional hurt that so frequently accompanies casual sex.

Abstinence is a reasonable and healthy strategy to adopt during certain periods of one's lifetime, e.g. during the emotionally and physically vulnerable teenage years, or it can be a goal to remain abstinent until in a lifelong committed relationship, i.e. marriage.

Here are some tips to help you to be abstinent:

- To start with, you need to believe in yourself: believe that you can practise abstinence, always being careful to avoid temptation.
- Then, it is important to communicate your decision to your boyfriend or girlfriend, so that you both know what is acceptable behaviour and what is not. Remember you can express your love in non-physical ways such as buying small gifts, being thoughtful, talking and laughing together.
- Finally, it is important to find support from family and friends, as the decision to practise abstinence can be tough, but it is certainly possible and, indeed, hugely beneficial.

There are many different factors that may play a role

in the decision to practise abstinence, e.g. religion, caring parents/guardians, a sense of personal maturity, the desire to gain control over future destiny. Whatever the reason, I would encourage you to consider the many benefits to being abstinent, realize that it is possible and a choice that is wholly yours to make.

Chapter 4

Solo Sex?
Masturbation

'Solo sex' is a good definition of masturbation because it sums up in just two words both the excitement and disappointment of it: the potential thrill of having sex without anyone else's needs to think about and the emptiness of not having anyone else to share it with.

Not that the disappointment is often mentioned. The advice on masturbation given on most teenage sexual advice websites can be summed up as, 'Masturbation is a normal, healthy and good way of exploring your body. It is not at all harmful no matter how often you do it, so it's fine to masturbate as often as you like.'

The Bible doesn't mention masturbation at all, so surely these websites are right and there can be nothing wrong with it? Well, actually the Bible does mention a lot of things which are relevant to frequent masturbation, such as holiness: being set apart from the crowd and distinctive like God himself (1 Thessalonians 4:7), self-control (Galatians 5:22–23), purity (1 Timothy 4:12) and denying self (Luke 9:23). Few Christians seem prepared to say that when they masturbate, they honestly do it for the glory of God.

Even secular culture occasionally betrays the possible emptiness of masturbation, too. In the film *American Beauty* (1999), we hear the principal character describe masturbating in the shower as the highlight of his day, very soon after his opening line of 'My name is Lester Burnham. I'm 42 years old. In less than a year, I'll be dead. In a way, I'm dead already.' I have heard many young Christians say that frequent masturbation makes them feel dead inside, too.

The hit show *Miss Saigon* has its opening sequence in a Saigon club frequented by GIs looking for girls to have a 'good time' with. In a moving soliloquy, one of the bar girls reveals her conflicting thoughts about her customers – nice on the outside but empty in their hearts. She recalls how impossible it is, however, to erase the painful 'movie in my mind', which gives the song its title.

Transformation of our thoughts is an important part of Christian maturity; the New Testament instructs us to be 'be transformed by the renewing of your mind' (Romans 12:2). The content of the 'movie in our mind' is very important at all times and no less so whilst masturbating. We are to think on those things that are pure as well as lovely (Philippians 4:8). In his Sermon on the Mount, Jesus himself warns us against lustful thoughts (Matthew 5:28) which can so easily become mental adultery or psychological rape.

Though the dangers outlined are very real, for most people, the state of anxiety and a disproportionate sense of guilt following masturbation can sometimes be as or more damaging than the masturbation itself. By the standard of scripture (even if church doctrine may differ) it is not a major issue. It can lead to sin and other sins may accompany it, but in itself, occasional masturbation may offer sexual release without sin.

Questions and Answers

1. What is masturbation? All my friends say they've done it.

Masturbation is having sex on your own by self-stimulating your genitals to achieve an orgasm. Doing this to someone else and/or them doing it to you is usually called mutual masturbation to distinguish it from solo sex.

A high percentage of boys will masturbate at some point in their lives. For boys, masturbation is often associated with using pornography. For girls, pornography use is much less common and masturbation itself is not as common as in boys.

2. People in our school talk about pulling off boys. What does this mean and how do you do it?

'Pulling a boy off' means stimulating him with your hands to give him sexual pleasure or an orgasm. This form of sexual activity is part of foreplay and usually eventually leads on to penetrative intercourse; it is therefore very risky if you are not planning to have full sex.

3. How many times can I masturbate a day? It normally takes me about seven to eight minutes. Is this normal for most guys?

The answer depends on why you are masturbating

this often. Sometimes masturbation is done quickly to relieve a surge of sexual tension and can be all over in less than a minute. At other times it can be a recurring pattern of behaviour which can consume hours of time each day.

What is much more important than the length of time it takes is how often you are doing it and how you feel afterwards.

Frequent daily or weekly masturbation can indicate loneliness, insecurity, sexual compulsion, or depression, from which masturbation may provide temporary relief but it does not solve the underlying problem. If you feel empty and unfulfilled after masturbation, then you may want to seek further help in exploring why.

It is also worth considering what kind of material (if any) you are using to stimulate the fantasies that you masturbate to. Often, whether television, video, DVD, Internet or magazine pictures are used, they present an airbrushed image which is not at all helpful in having a satisfying sexual relationship with a real person. Pornography is a recurrent cheat, promising the ultimate orgasm without being able to deliver it outside of the reality of personal intimacy.

4. I was wondering if STIs can be transferred if the boy masturbates the girl or vice versa?
Whilst solo sex does not transfer infection, even if there are warts on the hand, mutual masturbation

does permit this in the case of a few infections.

The two most likely to be transmitted in this way are herpes (HSV) and genital warts (caused by human papillomavirus). These two conditions are transmitted by skin-to-skin contact and can be transferred even with no visible spots or signs being present.

Many couples who engage in regular mutual masturbation, do however end up eventually having full intercourse, so it can be difficult in practice to prove whether an infection has been spread by mutual masturbation or because they have moved on to full intercourse.

5. I am a girl who masturbates quite a lot. Am I normal?
Although masturbation is not as common in girls as in boys, it does occur and you are quite normal.

But maybe as important as the masturbation are two related issues. Firstly, what you are thinking about during the masturbation itself. Thought patterns and subsequent sexual actions can become habit-forming. Are these thoughts and masturbation patterns making it easier or harder for you to delay sex with another person, if delaying is what you want to do? Alternatively, are they more likely to make you want to engage in early and possibly even casual sex?

Secondly, what unmet need is the masturbation

meeting? Much sexual activity is not so much about the desire to have sex but more about killing pain, craving for love or simply dealing with boredom, to take just a few examples. You may need to try to identify what is driving the frequent desire to masturbate and see if this need could be met in more appropriate ways

6. My boyfriend wants me to give him a wank but I don't know how to. How do I know how fast to go or how hard? Please don't laugh at me and please help.

Thanks for your question. Far from laughing at you, I am concerned that you should have to write to us about your boyfriend asking you to do this to him, when it seems that communication between the two of you is at such a low level that you have not (or could not have?) asked *him* this question. Masturbating your boyfriend, as he is requesting, is a very intimate sexual act and could well lead on to further more intimate behaviours, including full vaginal intercourse. Is that what you want?

I would be concerned that, as this is one way of reaching orgasm for him and since penetrative intercourse is more pleasurable for most men than masturbation, it will not be long before he is pressing you to go further.

You should also consider what masturbating him would do for you psychologically. Will it make you want to have sexual release in orgasm too? If so, how will you do this without risk of pregnancy or sexual infection? Do you know his previous sexual history and, in particular, how many partners he has had?

You should also know that there is a big difference between making love and having an orgasm. In doing this for him, are you making love to him and is it the kind of love you want now and will it last for the long-term future?

7. I was just wondering, is masturbation OK?

There are a lot of myths around masturbation, such as it makes you blind! These are totally untrue. Masturbation can temporarily relieve sexual tension and is sometimes successfully used by therapists to help patients with low sexual desire.

However, on the minus side of the equation, it can often leave you feeling inexplicably unfulfilled and often guilty, at least initially. Sex experts often struggle to explain this but I think it has its roots in the meaning of sex.

Sex is, first and foremost, a means of communication and not just recreation. At its very best, sex communicates the message 'I love you and am totally yours'. In solo sex, of course, this message can be an expression of self-centredness, rather than self-giving love.

If hours and hours of time are taken up with masturbating (as is often the case for boys and sometimes now for girls too), this can cause problems. Frequent masturbation is invariably linked with using pornography and this is potentially harmful in the long term as it depersonalizes sex, separating it from a real and meaningful relationship. Pornography is all about sexual pleasure without responsibility or commitment. Unfortunately, what you feed your mind on has a nasty habit of feeding on you eventually.

Masturbation of, or by, another person is a form of sexual climaxing and it can certainly run the risk of passing on sexually transmitted infection. Pregnancy, though, is highly unlikely, unless you move on to penetrative intercourse, which can easily happen in the heat of the moment.

8. I have heard people say that female masturbation can be associated with anxiety and guilt. Surely girls as well as boys need to explore their own bodies? We are in the twenty-first century now and have lots of STIs and pregnancy among teenagers. So tell me what is safer – to masturbate or to go around having sex in order to meet your sexual needs?

I do not think that it is helpful to encourage disproportionate concern over masturbation and you are right that STIs and pregnancy are much bigger problems if someone is having sex with others.

I would certainly not *teach* anyone to feel guilty

but the fact is that many, if not most people, do not
need to be taught to feel guilty about masturbation,
they just do feel this way. This is why they often seek
'permission' from a 'sex expert' to help them
overcome this guilt. Even those from very permis-
sive and liberal backgrounds feel this way
intuitively, at least initially.

Masturbation can become quite pattern-forming
and, particularly if associated with pornography,
can create an unhealthy expectation around sex and
relationships in the future.

It is important to be aware that there is an emotional side to any sexual activity; it is not just about
the physical experience and disease and pregnancy
avoidance. Self-esteem, self-awareness and self-
control are all interrelated. Understanding our
bodies, as you say, is very important, but so too is
being in control of our urges and drives rather than
allowing those passions to control us.

**9. Is it normal at my age (14) to get turned on by
looking at girls? I love masturbating but I want to
try to stop but can't. Can you help me please?**
It is quite normal for boys of your age to get sexually
excited by seeing girls. When you are a teenage boy,
it usually doesn't take much to get you turned on.
Most sex experts would agree that masturbation is
not physically harmful and usually it does no lasting
psychological harm either.

However, it can become compulsive, it is usually followed by a measure of guilt or at least dissatisfaction and it can never fulfil one of the main purposes of sex, which is to communicate loving commitment to another person. Masturbation is the sexual equivalent of talking to yourself – rarely the best way to have a good conversation!

As you have experienced, it can also be very difficult to stop. It is much easier if you have a trusted friend or adult with whom you can share the problem and have some kind of accountability.

Try to keep control of what you look at and think about. Avoiding pornography entirely will make controlling masturbation much easier. It is not always possible to prevent pornography coming looking for you but at least you can usually stop going searching for it, especially on the Internet.

Being in control in this area of your life will make it easier to be in control of your future sexual actions within relationships, and indeed in all other areas of your life.

Chapter 5

Quite A Catch?
Sexually Transmitted Infections

The *Washington Post* recently featured a typical comment on Christians and sexually transmitted infections (STIs as they are known in the UK, STDs in the USA where 'disease' replaces 'infection').

> Conservative Christian leaders and STDs are in many ways a natural match. Seen from a biblical mindset, the growing prevalence of STDs looks like the wages of sin, the price American society pays for the sexual revolution. And even medical experts agree that delaying sex until age 19 or 20 lowers the risk, and the only sure way to avoid ever contracting an STD is to be in a relationship where neither person has ever had another sexual partner.
> (www.washingtonpost.com/wp-dyn/content/article/2005/05/26/AR2005052601747.html)

The article is right in some ways. The Bible does say 'the wages of sin is death' (Romans 6:23) but STIs only occasionally result in death and more wages are paid overall on non-sexual sins which vastly out-number the sexual ones.

The Bible does however speak, in the Old Testament, of God punishing his people with a plague, that was probably of a sexually transmitted infection, resulting from the Israelites falling into sexual temptation, cunningly contrived by Balaam in an attempt to subvert the nation (Numbers 31:16). There is sometimes a specific link implied in the New Testament between sickness and personal sin (Matthew 9:2), but often this is an incorrect conclusion (John 9:2–3) and it is society as a whole that often pays the price of sexual license. Innocent victims, such as babies being infected with HIV from their mothers, suffer as much as the most promis-cuous drug abuser.

Another factor complicating the link between sexual sin and getting an STI, is the passage of time. Some sins are obvious, the New Testament tells us, but the consequences of some sins 'trail behind them' (1 Timothy 5:24) a long way. Some STIs, especially AIDS, may not become apparent for many years.

It is very important to recognize that though the Bible does not teach that sexual sins are the worst kind, they are a specific type of sin in that 'he who sins sexually sins against his own body'

(1 Corinthians 6:18). STIs are just one possible out-working of that.

The psychological consequences of having an STI can be devastating. With STI rates at an all-time high in the UK, especially among teenagers, knowing the previous sexual history of your partner and being able to trust that their account is true, is absolutely essential. With several studies showing infection rates just for chlamydia are running at 10 per cent in the sexually active teenage population, it is no wonder than many experts are now saying that safe sex is much more to do with the safety of your partner than whether you use a condom or not. Once again, waiting until marriage for an uninfected partner can save a lot of heartache.

Questions and Answers

1. My partner had sex before we met. She only had it once. Could she have got infected then?
Unfortunately, if her partner at that time had an STI, she could have picked up an infection too.

If she and her previous partner used condoms correctly, they could have reduced the risk but they would not have completely removed the risk of, for example, genital warts or herpes. Some infections have a long incubation period and some may be present for years without any symptoms, especially chlamydia.

For your peace of mind, and hers, it would be a good thing for you both to be tested for STIs at the Genito-Urinary Medicine (GUM) or STI (Sexually Transmitted Infection) clinic in your local hospital, or with your own GP. If you are both clear of infection, and remain faithful to each other lifelong, then you can relax about the possibility of STIs in the future.

2. Can I get sexual diseases if I use a condom?
The condom is one of the most effective contraceptives at reducing the chance of STI transmission. Even so, STIs may still be spread. For example, studies have shown that wearing a condom reduces the risk of getting HIV from an infected partner by 85 per cent but this still leaves a 15 per cent risk.

Condoms do not prevent transmission of viruses such as human papillomavirus (HPV) which can spread by skin-to-skin contact from areas not covered by the condom.

3. Do genital warts hurt? Do they have a colour or smell? Can they be cured and how do you know if you have warts without having to go to a clinic?

Genital warts are caused by infection with human papillomavirus and are the commonest viral sexually transmitted infection in the UK. They are usually colourless or white and can vary in size from a pinhead to large crops of warts covering much of the vulva or penis.

The warts do not smell but STIs often occur together, so warts can be caught along with other STIs which do cause a smelly discharge. Larger ones can be easily diagnosed, as they look much like warts elsewhere. Smaller ones can be difficult. They can be diagnosed by GPs and some GPs would be prepared to instruct you in home treatment with *podophyllotoxin*, (not *podophyllin* which is not suitable for home treatment). However, if there is doubt about the diagnosis or if another infection may also be present, then visiting a GU specialist in a hospital clinic is best.

You should also know that condoms offer little or no protection against HPV transmission, so anyone with warts will remain at risk of spreading the infection after treatment, even if condoms are used consistently, i.e. properly on every occasion.

4. What is herpes? Is there a cure for it?

There are two types of herpes infection (herpes simplex virus) – HSV1 and HSV2. HSV1 usually infects the mouth and surrounding area and HSV2 the genital area. However, with oral sex, the two types of virus often infect both areas.

In a first-time infection with either virus, there are multiple painful small blisters which break out over the infected area. Other symptoms of genital herpes may include lymph node enlargement in the groin, fever and pain on passing urine.

Herpes viruses travel down the nerve roots that supply the area of infected skin and remain there for life. There they lie dormant but can be reactivated at any time. The currently available treatments in the form of creams to rub on the skin (topical) or tablets (systemic) all interfere with the multiplication of the virus but do not eradicate it. In severe or frequently recurring cases, the tablets can reduce the severity or frequency of attacks.

Herpes can be passed on and picked up even when someone has no visible sores, as the virus is passed on by skin-to-skin contact. Because the virus can be present over all the genital skin, condoms are not very effective.

5. What diseases cause the inside of the vagina to inflame and itch, and sex to be painful? Could this be cystitis?

Cystitis is an infection of the bladder and usually causes burning on passing urine and the desire to pass urine often (frequency).

The symptoms you describe are more in keeping with an infection of the vagina itself. Such infections cause redness and soreness of the vagina, which is often worse during intercourse, and there may also be a discharge from the vagina.

Thrush or candidiasis is a very common cause of vaginal inflammation and is not necessarily sexually transmitted. However, other sexually transmitted bacterial infections can cause these symptoms too and you should get this checked out with your GP or at a GUM clinic. This is because some infection can spread from the vagina to your fallopian tubes and lead to infertility in later life.

If you have never had sex, however, thrush is the most likely cause and is usually effectively treated with pessaries (vaginal tablets) and creams which can be obtained from a pharmacy or from your GP.

6. I had oral sex and lots of body contact with someone on Saturday and am now itching a lot in my genital area as well as the rest of my body. I think I

**may have got pubic lice. Can you advise me on what
to do?**

There are two common parasitic infestations which
can be spread by the kind of intimate contact you
describe.

One, as you say, is pubic lice. They infect the pubic
and axillary (armpit) hair, and occasionally the
eyelashes, eyebrows and any bearded area of the
face. Both the lice and their eggs (nits) can be seen
with the naked eye. Treatment for lice, such as
malathion, can be bought over the counter at a
pharmacy and must be applied to all hairy areas
except the scalp.

The other infection is scabies. This mite causes
intense itching all over the body. Burrows of the mite
can often be seen in the finger webs and armpits.
The treatment for scabies is covering the entire body
from the neck down with an agent such as *lindane
1 per cent solution*. Even when the treatment is
successful, the itch can take weeks to go.

Scabies mites can survive up to three days off the
body and so potentially contaminated clothes and
bedding should be either discarded or washed at
high temperature (above 50°C). Where there is one
STI, there may well be another and whether scabies
or lice are the cause, you should get a check-up at a
GUM clinic. Oral sex is still sexual intercourse and
can lead to a transmission of a wide range of STIs.

7. I had a smear test six months ago and it said that HPV had been found. But when I had another one, it was no longer detected and I was told not to worry. Could the result of my smear be incorrect the second time?

You should not be unduly worried about this. Mildly abnormal smears (sometimes referred to as 'inflammatory smears') are very common and the majority, as in your case, revert back to normal. HPV infection is very common among sexually active men and women. There are more than eighty types of HPV, the majority of which are cleared by the immune system with time.

Some types of HPV infection do however cause cervical pre-cancer and cancer. It is therefore very important that you continue to have regular smears as advised by your own doctor or clinic.

8. Should I be vaccinated against HPV and will I still need smears after vaccination?

The current Department of Health recommendation is that all girls should be vaccinated against HPV and the course of three injections needed for this should be started at age 12. This is because the vaccine works best (and may only work at all) when given *before* HPV infection has occurred 10% of girls are already infected by the age of 16. The vaccine is highly effective in preventing infection with HPV types 16 and 18, the two types which cause 70% or more of cancers of the cervix. However, there are two important points to remember about HPV vaccine. The HPV vaccine only partially protects against one STI. There are many more than this and you should know your partner's sexual history and if you are not both virgins you should use a condom. You should also continue to have regular smears after you begin having sexual intercourse because the vaccine does not protect against all cervical cancers and the length of time for which the vaccine may be effective is currently uncertain. Booster vaccinations may need to be given later in adult life.

9. I have recently been diagnosed with chlamydia. I am 14 and have been having sex with my boyfriend. Is chlamydia caught from body fluids or from skin-to-skin?

Chlamydia is a bacterial infection and is now the most common STI in the UK. In some cities, around 10 to 15 per cent of sexually active women may be infected. The infection is important because in most cases, in both men and women, there are no symptoms and the disease can remain undetected for years.

In men, it can cause a discharge or swelling of the testes. In women it can cause irregular periods and a burning sensation when passing urine (dysuria). It is a more serious infection in women because of three important complications:

- It is a common cause of infertility as it damages the fallopian tubes.
- It is associated with a higher risk of cervical cancer.
- It can cause severe abdominal pain if it infects the fallopian tubes.

Chlamydia is an organism that lives within human cells. It is transmitted by fluids and not skin-to-skin contact. Despite this, there is little evidence that condoms offer reliable protection from chlamydia infection. Consistent condom use seems to halve the rate of infection but by no means eliminates it altogether.

Also, remember that sex under the age of 16 is illegal in Great Britain; in Northern Ireland the age of consent is 17.

I would be very concerned that at only 14 years old you are making the choice to have sex. You have your whole life ahead of you and the impact of early sex on your future is massive. Not only are you at risk of further infections but teenage pregnancy and emotional hurt can easily result from the choice to have sex at a young age. It is worth reviewing your choices for the future, ideally with a parent or an adult you can trust. You are a very special person and it is never too late to make different sexual choices the next time.

10. My vagina is very swollen and painful. At the start, there was a yellow discharge. I have also got a lot of pain when I pass water and in my back. I've been to the doctors about this over the past eighteen weeks but have only been given antibiotics for a water infection. What should I do?

My first thought is around the possibility of you having picked up a sexually transmitted infection. Have you had sex or been sexually intimate with another person? Did you practise 'safe sex'? Remember that even if condoms are used consistently they only reduce the risk rather than removing it.

Many STI symptoms such as back pain and pain on passing water (dysuria) also occur with urine infections but this would not account for a yellow discharge and the vaginal swelling.

Several infections cause an abnormal discharge. A yellow one is typical of infection with an organism called trichomonas vaginale, though other infective causes of discharge are chlamydia, bacterial vaginosis and gonorrhoea.

Occasionally non-infective causes, such as allergy to vaginal cosmetics or medicines, can cause swelling in the vagina. You should get a check-up as soon as possible. If you would find it difficult to go back to your GP again about this problem you could visit a local GUM clinic.

11. I have just found out from a swab test that I have chlamydia. My partner and I are now on antibiotics to clear it up. I have a major concern that it will affect my having children. Can I have a test that will tell me?

One of the complications of chlamydia infection is that it can ascend from the vagina into the fallopian tubes and cause pelvic inflammatory disease (PID). It is this complication of chlamydia that is associated with infertility. Just one episode of PID is thought to lead to fertility problems in around 10 per cent of cases but after three attacks of PID, this rises rapidly to 70 per cent or more. Gonorrhoea is another infection leading to high infertility rates and sometimes two or more infections are caught together.

In your case, I think the outlook is very optimistic, though you should of course be very careful not to get another infection and stay faithful to an uninfected partner. Using condoms may also help to reduce the risk of chlamydia infection but it does not eliminate it.

With regard to tests, gynaecologists can carry out a test called a 'lap and dye' to check that the tubes are not blocked. This involves putting a telescope device called a laparoscope into the tummy whilst you are under anaesthetic. A dye is introduced into the neck of the womb and if at least one tube is not blocked, the dye will trickle out into the abdomen and be seen through the laparoscope. This type of test is only advisable if you experience difficulty in conceiving as it does involve some risk.

Recent research shows that chalmydia infection can make men infertile too, so your boyfriend may also need investigation if you want to have children together in the future.

12. I have had anal sex with my girlfriend. A friend of hers told her that this type of sex has a high risk of AIDS. Is this true?

The risk of getting a sexually transmitted disease from penetrative anal sex (whether hetero- or homosexual) is much higher than from vaginal sex, even when using a condom. Without a condom, anal sex is an even more high-risk behaviour. However, the risk of transmission of diseases such as hepatitis B is much greater than that of AIDS and if having anal sex, you should both consider getting vaccinated against hepatitis B.

AIDS is still quite uncommon among the white, exclusively heterosexual population in the UK, but most experts consider the risk of AIDS transmission from an infected female to be thirty times greater from anal sex than from vaginal. It is a low risk if the female does not abuse drugs, come from a high-risk geographical area (such as East Africa) and has never had sex with other men in high-risk groups (such as intravenous drug users, gay men and bisexuals, and those from sub-Saharan Africa or South East Asia).

Anal sex can lead to serious injury to your girlfriend's anal sphincter and also increase her risk of getting anal cancer when she is older. The lining of the rectum is very delicate, easily torn and full of faecal material, which can cause many infections. In short, it was not designed for sexual intercourse and anal intercourse should be avoided.

13. I had oral sex and realize now that an STI could have been transmitted. What symptoms would I get? I have a sore throat. Would a doctor be able to tell the difference if it were caused by an STI? If semen was swallowed, would I be able to contract HIV and how likely is this?

You are quite right that a wide variety of STIs can be passed on through oral sex. The symptoms depend on the type of infection. Gonorrhoea for example may give a sore throat but may give no symptoms. Genital herpes infection will give tiny painful ulcers or blisters in the mouth and on the tongue. Syphilis is a very serious STI which is increasing at an alarming rate in the UK at present. Its most common mode of transmission is through oral sex. A painless ulcer (chancre) can occur anywhere around the mouth or on the facial area around the chin, cheeks and lips.

It is currently thought that HIV can be passed on by oral sex though this is very rare. It is obviously very important for you to know your partner's HIV status and their risk of having HIV. If they have never had sex with any other man or sex with anyone from high-risk ethnic groups from Africa,

Asia or East Europe or with drug users, then the risk to you is very small. This emphasizes the vital importance of knowing a partner and their sexual history really well before having any intimate sexual activity such as oral sex.

Finally, it is important to be aware that oral sex is sex. Some young people today think that because pregnancy will not occur then it is safer. They forget about the STI risks and the obvious emotional impact, which is often as great as in a teenage relationship involving vaginal sex. Often, too, oral sex leads on to vaginal sex with associated pregnancy risks. Think through clearly all your relationship choices as they do have massive implications for you now and in the future.

14. Can you be tested for all STIs including HIV at a GP surgery or a family planning clinic?
You can be tested for some of the common STIs at either a GP surgery or a family planning clinic.

Chlamydia testing is increasingly available and involves a fine swab being inserted into the cervical and urethral openings in women and into the urethra in men. More recently, chlamydia infection can be tested for on urine specimens also, which is easier to collect. Other STIs such as gonorrhoea can also be detected from swabs.

Blood tests can also be carried out for infections such as syphilis and HIV. Three months should elapse between the last risk of exposure and performing the most commonly used test for HIV antibodies, as the antibodies can take this length of time to develop. Swabs will usually have to be transported from a GP surgery or family planning clinic to be processed and this can result in problems in getting the most accurate results.

On-site testing in a GUM clinic is probably best, if there is one close by, as a wider range of STIs can be tested for and microscopy, if needed, can be carried out there and then in the clinic. If you have put yourself at risk, then it is important to be tested.

15. I have a whole lot of little white bumps on my penis and hair seems to be growing out of them. I keep thinking I have HPV. The bumps are more on the base of my penis and the scrotum. What are they?
This question is one of the most common we are asked. A lot of teens worry about spots on their penis and they are a frequent cause of attendance at GUM clinics. Around half of those attending a GUM clinic do not have an STI and I am sure you are among those that don't too.

What you describe sound like the normal hair follicles and grease glands that cover the genital area. Another common cause of worry is pearly penile papules which are tiny white spots that form a ring or fringe around the edge of the glans of the penis (bell-end).

HPV is a very common disease, however, and can be transmitted even with consistent condom use, so you should get the spots checked out by a doctor if you have ever had genital sexual contact.

16. I have a rash that's always itching on the side of my penis and scrotum. It's constantly red. What could it be?
There are a number of skin diseases, such as eczema and psoriasis, which can affect most areas of the body including the genital area. However, a common cause of an itching red rash in the groin is ringworm. This is a fungal infection which if untreated can spread right down the inner thigh and leg.

The treatment is with an anti-fungal cream such as *miconazole*, which can be bought from a chemist or prescribed by your GP. It should be applied twice a day. A large area of ringworm can take many weeks or even months of applying the cream to clear.

If you have been sexually active or think you may be at risk of having an STI then this should be checked out, but from your description the rash does not sound as if it is a sign of an STI.

17. I've had trich before. At first I didn't know that I had it until the discharge started coming all the time. I threw up after taking the pills I was given, but afterwards felt better and the discharge stopped.

About five or six months after this the discharge started again. Is it normal to discharge at all?

Trichomonas vaginale (trich or TV) is a protozoan infection that gives no symptoms in half of women and over three-quarters of infected men. In women, the symptoms are usually a thin, yellow frothy discharge that smells unpleasant. Mild itching and pain on intercourse may also occur.

The treatment for trich is usually a course of an antibiotic called *metronidazole* which is probably what you had, since it does often make people feel nauseous when they take it.

Vaginal discharge can be a normal event and if your current discharge is not typical of TV it may be that this is normal for you. However, it is possible that the original infection was not eliminated by the course of antibiotics you had previously, or if you have had sex with an infected partner subsequent to treatment, you may be re-infected. I would certainly advise you to go back to the doctor who treated you originally to be tested again.

18. What symptoms would you have if you got gonorrhoea in your throat?

Oral transmission of gonorrhoea often gives no symptoms at all but pharyngitis (inflamed sore throat) may occur.

Gonorrhoea is highly infectious and a single sexual act results in passing it on in more than 50 per cent of cases. If the disease is not detected and treated at an early stage, it can go on to give severe complications such as abscesses, and infertility in women from tubal damage. Though all rare, arthritis, damage to the heart and even meningitis can result too. You are also highly likely to pass the disease on to other sexual partners even if you have no symptoms at present.

If you have been at risk of getting gonorrhoea, it is most important to get checked out by a GUM clinic or GP.

19. How soon after intercourse can STIs be detected?
The incubation period (the time from being infected to the development of symptoms) varies a great deal. For the commoner bacterial infections, the incubation period is generally shorter than for viral infections. For chlamydia, it takes from one to three weeks and for gonorrhoea, two to ten days. It takes around two to six weeks for the ulcer of primary syphilis to appear.

For genital herpes (HSV) it usually takes between two and ten days for blisters to develop, though occasionally up to three weeks. For genital warts (HPV) the usual incubation period is one to three months but it can be much longer.

HIV antibodies take up to three months before they can reliably be detected by the current standard tests.

Anyone who has put themselves at risk of picking

up a sexually transmitted infection should attend their own doctor or a GUM clinic to be tested.

20. Where do you go to get tested for STIs, what do they do, and do your former sexual partners get informed if you are infected?

STIs are very common in teenagers. Around one in ten sexually active teenagers are infected with chlamydia, for example, and this commonly gives no symptoms. Some of the complications of chlamydia can be serious and other infections such as HIV and syphilis can be fatal.

Obviously it is important to trace sexual partners if you have such an infection and patients are encouraged to speak to and encourage their sexual partners to attend themselves.

However, GPs have a duty of confidentiality to you which would only be broken in the most exceptional of circumstances, such as threat to the life of another person. However, having an STI is very serious and especially if you are a younger teen living at home, doctors have a duty to encourage you to tell a parent or guardian, unless there were overwhelming reasons why you should not. Though most parents/ guardians would initially be upset, once this has settled they are generally in the best position to give you the ongoing support that you may need.

GUM clinics have special contact tracing arrangements whereby they can inform your previous sexual partners that they may be at risk and invite them to come for screening, without revealing your identity.

You can usually find the address and contact number of your local GUM clinic on the Web, in the local telephone directory or through asking your GP surgery. You may have to make an appointment or you may be able to just attend without one.

Staff are trained to be helpful and non-judgmental and will ask you to give details of your symptoms and sexual history. They will examine you, take swabs and blood tests, and arrange treatment and follow-up for you. It is important to attend follow-up visits, even if you feel well, as further tests may have to be done to ensure that you are cured or to minimize your future risk if you are not free from disease.

Chapter 6

Playing Safe?
Contraception and Pregnancy

Contraception is now widely accepted as the obvious solution to the problem of enabling sex to occur without the complication of pregnancy. In fact, many sexual health experts would see it as the only solution. Jesus, however, taught us that 'wisdom is shown to be right by what results from it' (Matthew 11:19, NLT). If contraception is the solution to unplanned pregnancy, how is it that the UK has the highest unplanned pregnancy rate in Western Europe and our abortion rates in the UK increase year on year and recently topped 200,000 a year for the first time?

Reproduction was certainly one of the purposes of God in designing sex and Genesis 1:28 is often seen as a command to multiply. However, this text is a blessing, not a command. 'God blessed them and

said to them, "Be fruitful and increase in number."'
This does not decree what humans must do but
describes what God does through humankind.
Nowhere does scripture indicate that every act of
sexual intercourse has to have reproduction as its
primary or even a possible goal. Contraception is
not intrinsically wrong for Christians, though
different wings of the Christian Church have their
own deeply-held perspectives on the issue.
However, even for Christians who do not rule out
the use of contraception entirely, its widespread
availability and promotion in the UK over more than
thirty years poses at least two other major questions
to consider.

Firstly, several methods of contraception such as
the coil (IUD) and many types of pill (especially
progestogen-only pills) may prevent implantation
rather than fertilization. Many would consider this a
very early abortion and, as the Bible clearly indicates
God's care for, and involvement with, the unborn
(e.g. Psalm 139, Luke 1:44), such methods of
contraception may be ethically unacceptable. Even
when there is uncertainty about the status of
prenatal life, surely life should always be given the
benefit of the doubt? Those who share God's
priorities are to 'speak up for those who cannot
speak for themselves' (Proverbs 31:8) and this
includes the unborn.

Secondly, those methods, such as condoms, which
clearly do prevent fertilization, are not without

problems either. Inconsistent or incorrect use is common, especially among teenagers. Even when used correctly, condoms have up to a 15 per cent failure rate. We would say condoms only usually delay getting pregnant – they certainly do not prevent it when used long term. Also the availability of condoms may indirectly increase unplanned pregnancy by encouraging those in two minds about whether to have first sex or not, to do so in the mistaken belief that they will be safe. In the UK, over three quarters of unplanned pregnancies in teenagers are in those using contraception.

Questions and Answers

1. My boyfriend and I are truly in love with each other and, only recently, began to have sex. I worry about pregnancy and I always check the condom after he ejaculates but is it possible that a condom can leak?

An intact condom which does not slip and is carefully applied and removed does not leak, but condoms can often split, slip or be used incorrectly and they are one of the least reliable methods of contraception, especially when used by younger teenagers.

The failure rate of condoms in preventing pregnancy in this age group is around 15 per cent. This means that each year 15 out of every 100 females using condoms for contraception will become pregnant. Also, a condom does not protect against all sexually transmitted infections.

I am glad that you are involved with a boy that you truly love but I would encourage you to reassess the physical side of your relationship. Clearly you rightly do not feel ready for pregnancy and yet the reality is no method of contraception will guarantee you 100 per cent protection from this. You are obviously facing a lot of stress having to 'always check the condom' and I am sure you are watching every month for your period, too. Is it worth it, where you are in life at present?

Many people later regret getting involved sexually too early in a relationship and if your boyfriend really cares about you, he will be prepared to wait with you until you are properly committed to each other and fear of pregnancy would not be an issue.

You should tell him it is stressful having sex when you are constantly worrying that you might become pregnant. All the risks and fears are minimized if you wait until you have made a lifelong commitment to each other before having sex.

2. I would like more information on the pill? How long does it work for? How do you use it? When should it be taken? Where can I get it?

There are two main types of the pill: the combined oral contraceptive (COC) which contains two hormones (an oestrogen and a progestogen) and the progestogen-only pill (POP) which, as its name suggests, contains only the progestogen.

The COC is the most popular and is the most effective. It is usually taken for three weeks at a time with a pill-free interval of one week during which a withdrawal bleed, like a period, usually occurs. The COC is only obtainable on prescription from your GP or a family planning clinic, who offer a completely confidential service. However, sharing with at least one parent/guardian your decision to take the pill is a wise idea, as it is a very important life choice with many possible consequences. Though severe side effects and complications from taking the COC are rare, your blood pressure will need to be checked every six months, and taking the COC and smoking regularly can increase your risk of developing a blood clot. This risk increases with age.

Many COCs work principally by preventing ovulation and as long as pills are not missed, it is reliable in preventing pregnancy. However, COCs do not prevent STIs and can increase the risk of getting some infections such as chlamydia.

The POP is also only available on prescription but does not carry the risks posed by oestrogens in the COC. It works by preventing either fertilization or implantation. It has to be taken at around the same time every day. It may offer some protection against pelvic infection because of its effect of thickening cervical mucus.

With both the COC and POP, some advance planning is needed in preventing pregnancy. Though some types of COC are effective immediately if taken on the first day of your period, it is as well to be on the pill for at least a month to ensure its maximum effectiveness. There is also a moral dimension around contraception and for some people one or all methods may be unacceptable.

3. I use the pill but suffer badly from depression when I am taking it. Which hormone in the pill makes you feel depressed and would the mini-pill or implants solve the problem?
The link with depression and the hormonal content

of the pill is not well supported by medical research but in practice, of course, taking the pill has all sorts of psychological and moral implications which could lead to depression, especially in younger girls where research has shown that two thirds have regrets about their first sexual intercourse.

The mini-pill (POP) contains only one hormone and some women do feel more relaxed with this pill, since it carries less risk of raised blood pressure or clots.

The only contraceptive hormonal implant available currently in the UK releases a progestogen only. There is, again, no evidence that the implant causes depression but the lifestyle and psychological factors that contribute to women's choice of this particular method may be relevant to vulnerability to depression.

Mood swings with periods with or without taking the pill can certainly be very troublesome and you may need to seek further help from your GP if the symptoms of depression are persistent.

As always, it is worth considering whether there are any other factors in your life that might be contributing to your feelings and, in particular, whether you are comfortable with your relationship and the current degree of physical intimacy with respect to your plans for the future.

4. I am 15, have been in a steady relationship for over a year now and am very happy. I had sex after two months, as I thought I was ready and I was happy. I still am, and continue to have sex. First I used condoms, then I went on the pill. I feel safe, as I never fail to take it. As my period is very scanty, I continue to have sex the seven days that I'm not on the pill after the three weeks. Does the pill cover this period?

The pill should provide contraceptive cover for the complete duration of the cycle including the seven pill-free days. However, you are probably aware that no contraceptive is 100 per cent effective. Even though, when taken regularly, the pill failure rate is very low, if you have, for example, a tummy bug or if you are given a course of antibiotics, this can stop the pill from working properly.

I assume the doctor who prescribes the pill for you has discussed the different side effects with you – particularly if you are a smoker too. There is an increased risk of clots in the veins in women on the pill and, though rare, you should report any swelling or pain in your calves or sudden chest pain or breathlessness. Some users find the pill can bring on migraine or make them worse. It is important to have your blood pressure and weight checked regularly as the pill can affect these.

Though you say that you felt ready to have sex, you may not be aware that the risk of cervical cancer in later life is increased in girls who start sex at an early age. They are also more vulnerable to catching an STI, since the covering (epithelium) of the neck of the womb is not fully mature.

I notice also that you say you do not use condoms now. If you continue having sex, you should remember that the pill provides no protection against STIs and can actually increase the risk of some. Whilst condoms do not protect against all STIs they do give considerable protection against some.

A lot of really good 'in love' teenage relationships do not survive the test of time and although I hope yours does, you must consider whether you would want to develop a sexual side to your next relationship so early as in this one. Without intention, young people can have had multiple partners before they leave their teens, as a result of having sex with a number of successive partners in 'in love' relationships. This obviously can leave them vulnerable to STIs, unplanned pregnancy and emotional hurt.

Moreover, because you are 15, your boyfriend is actually breaking the law as, in Great Britain, the age of consent for sex is 16 or 17 in Northern Ireland. You may want to talk over these things with him, and I would encourage you even now to reconsider and wait until you are older and have made a lifelong commitment to a partner. Having regular sex with your boyfriend now is likely to make it much more difficult to form a committed and exclusive sexual relationship later on.

5. Does taking the pill increase my chances of getting cancer?

The short answer is that taking the pill for many years does slightly increase the risk of getting cancer of the cervix and breast cancer. Research currently indicates the risk of getting ovarian cancer may be reduced in those who take the pill.

The pill is usually taken when starting to have sex, and having sex at an early age is strongly linked with an increased risk of cervical cancer. The reason for this is that cervical cancer is caused by changes in the cells linked with human papillomavirus (HPV) infection, which is the commonest viral STI. Infection with HPV usually gives no symptoms and the person you have sex with may not know they have it. The younger you start having sex, the more likely you are to get HPV infection.

6. Before I have sex with my boyfriend I plan to go on the pill, but I also plan to use a condom during sexual intercourse. What are the risks of getting pregnant even when using both types of contraception? (Female, 15)

It is good to think ahead and it is good to be able to communicate in a relationship about these things, and even better if you can openly discuss such important decisions with a parent or guardian.

Obviously using both the pill and the condom will reduce the risk of pregnancy more than using either on its own and, in this situation, the risk of pregnancy is very low. However, the younger you are when you start having sex, the more likely you are to have more than one sexual relationship and having multiple partners (albeit one at a time) means it is more likely that you will get an STI.

Remember that you are at risk from an STI even if you use a condom, unless you are only having sex with someone who has never had sex with anyone else before. Sex and love are not the same thing. Love has to do with respect, trust, honesty and commitment, and so many other characteristics of a good friendship. At your age, it is very likely that the relationship you have now will not last, as it is very difficult to maintain the level of commitment required when young. Also, if you do have sex, the relationship is more and more likely to focus on this physical aspect and not on the friendship side of things. You may well ultimately feel used and the rejection will be that much more intense if the relationship breaks up. People lose self-esteem when they give such an intimate part of themselves and then it doesn't work out.

Sex is very special and it is so easy to make a decision to start sex and then have regrets later. Sex made you and you are special, as is your boyfriend. Treat each other with the respect you deserve and demand respect for yourself from your relationships, both now and in the future. Don't let sex confuse your feelings.

7. What is the morning-after pill and where can I get it? Also, does it cost a lot? I don't really understand the way it works.

The morning after pill (MAP), also known as the emergency pill, can be taken up to seventy-two hours after sex (and possibly up to five days according to the latest research), to try and prevent pregnancy occurring.

It consists of two tablets each containing 750 micrograms of the progestogen *levonorgestrel*. Both tablets are taken together and the sooner after intercourse this is done, the more effective it is in preventing pregnancy.

Early in the menstrual cycle the MAP may work by preventing ovulation and/or fertilization but later in the cycle its main effects are in preventing implantation of the fertilized egg in the lining of the uterus. If it fails to prevent pregnancy, however, there is no evidence that it will harm the developing baby. There are obviously, therefore, because of a possible post-fertilization action, moral implications for some people to consider depending on their own personal moral perspective.

The MAP can be obtained free of charge from your GP, a family planning clinic or many hospital casualty departments. It can also be purchased from chemists and currently costs around £20.

It is important to realize that, by definition, girls seeking to take the MAP have had unprotected sex and are also at risk of getting a sexual infection.

Around 10 per cent of young women using MAP are infected with chlamydia. MAP offers no protection against STIs, so if you need to use it, it is sensible to be tested for chlamydia a few weeks after intercourse has taken place. This can be arranged by your GP or GUM (genito-urinary) clinic and some larger pharmacies.

Obviously it is important to consider how past sexual choices have or could have impacted on your future. MAP may seem to some young people as an easy way to prevent the consequences of an unplanned sexual encounter or failed contraception. The reality is, it was never intended by the manufacturers for regular use, and sex has not only pregnancy and possible infection but also emotional, psychological and spiritual implications.

8. How do contraceptive injections work and how long have they been used for?

Injections of progestogen hormones have been used for over thirty years now in more than one hundred countries around the world.

It is a very effective method of contraception with a failure rate of less than 1 per cent each year when given regularly every twelve weeks. It works largely by stopping the ovaries from releasing an egg each month, as well as thickening the mucus from the cervix and making it more difficult for sperm to get through. It also makes the lining of the womb thinner and so less likely for any fertilized egg to implant.

It can have an unpredictable effect on periods. At first, bleeding may be heavier than usual and the period may last longer. Periods may become irregular and often stop altogether. This is not exactly helpful if you are very worried about becoming pregnant.

Also, the injection gives little or no protection against STIs so, unless you are in a lifelong, faithful sexual relationship with a non-infected partner, doctors would recommend that you should use condoms to give at least some protection against the risk of being infected with one.

9. I have heard that you can't get pregnant the first time you have sex. Is this true?

There are many myths and 'old wives tales' that circulate among young people about pregnancy that are very misleading such as:

- You can't get pregnant if you do it standing up.
- You can't get pregnant if you jump up and down immediately after sex.
- You can't get pregnant if you use contraception. (All contraception has failure rates.)
- You can't get pregnant the first time you have sex.

The simple answer to your question is 'No'. You *can*

get pregnant the first time you have sex. In fact, it is possible to get pregnant any time you have sex and that includes having sex during a girl's period.

10. If I have sex with my girlfriend during her period, can she still get pregnant?

This simple answer to your question is yes your girlfriend could get pregnant if you have sex with her during her period, but it would be rare that this would happen.

In theory, there are only two or three fertile days every month for women in which pregnancy can occur, but in practice, because of many factors, such as irregular periods, it can be hard to know when these days are and therefore they are hard to predict exactly.

The reason a woman has her period is because there is no fertilized egg to plant in the womb lining. Ovulation (release of the egg) is the primary event and not menstruation (period blood loss) which happens 14 days after ovulation.

If your girlfriend has a short cycle of, say, 21 days, this means she ovulates on day 7, straight after or possibly just during, the end of her period. Your sperm may live for up to a week after intercourse and hence having sex during her period, especially (but not only) in short cycle, can lead to conception occurring.

I hope you can take all of that in. It sure is a lot to fully understand but basically all you need to remember is, *yes it is possible* to get your girlfriend pregnant during her period.

11. Is there any way you can be pregnant and still have your period?
In answer to your question, let me explain a bit about periods. After an egg is released from a woman's ovaries, it passes down the fallopian tube towards the womb. During this time the womb lining becomes thicker and softer in order for a fertilized egg to become implanted and to grow. However, if the egg is not fertilized, this thick lining of the womb is shed and results in a period.

So as you can now see, a girl would be very unlikely to be pregnant if she had a period because there is nowhere for the fertilized egg to grow. I say very *unlikely* because the strangest things sometimes happen, and sometimes a pregnancy can occur outside the womb and also a woman can bleed early in a pregnancy in the womb, which might possibly be confused with a period. This type of bleed early in pregnancy is referred to as an 'implantation bleed', which means that the embryo has embedded in the uterus but the lining from the rest of the uterus has been shed.

In general, though, you do not have your period when you are pregnant. If someone is in doubt over whether they are pregnant, they should get a pregnancy test done.

12. I think I'm pregnant. I'm afraid to tell anyone about it. What should I do? I can't tell my parents they would be so disappointed.

I can tell from your question that you are very distressed and I will try to help you as best I can.

First of all you must confirm whether or not you are pregnant. The easiest way to tell if you are pregnant is to do a pregnancy test. It is important to remember that it may show negative if done too soon, so it would be advisable to talk to your doctor. You can buy pregnancy test kits from chemist shops but it is always a good idea to have it done somewhere you can talk about the result to someone who is used to talking about pregnancy issues, such as your doctor or a trained counsellor at a crisis pregnancy centre (contact details in phone book). You could take a friend along with you for support if you wished.

Feeling you might be pregnant when you hadn't planned it, is definitely a scary experience to go through. If you are pregnant, don't be afraid to tell your parents/guardians. They may be shocked at first, but most parents/guardians care more than anyone else would for you, will always have your best interests at heart and are in the best position to help you through the pregnancy and afterwards.

Whether you are pregnant or not, I hope you will have learned from this experience. Remember how worried you are now feeling and how easily pregnancy can happen. Remember, where we go and what we achieve in our lives depends on choices we make today.

13. I have been going out with my girlfriend for nearly six months now and we are having sex. I'm really worried that she might get pregnant. What should I do?
You are certainly wise to be concerned about pregnancy as it is a really big issue and could happen very easily.

You don't mention anything about your views/ use of contraception, including your personal moral views. Remember, contraception reduces risk but pregnancy can still occur. Even if condoms are being used properly every time without any accidents, pregnancies still do occur. All forms of contraception have failure rates and it is important to realize that failure is more likely to happen among younger, inexperienced users.

Setting aside the issue of pregnancy for a moment, you have also exposed yourself and your girlfriend to the risk of sexually transmitted infections if either of you have been sexually active before. You would need to get checked out at the genito-urinary (GUM) or STI clinic in your local hospital, or with your own GP.

I would encourage you to talk to your girlfriend and let her know how you feel. Talk through what you would do if your girlfriend got pregnant? What would your families and friends think? What would it mean at school and for your future career? Are you ready for a baby? Do you want to run the risk of picking up an STI? Though an abortion is considered by some an easy way out, it is not – and do you really want the first child you father to end up as an abortion statistic?

Finally, if this relationship ends at some stage in the future, think through whether you want sex to enter the equation so early in your next relationship. Remember you are in control of these things and it is good to talk it through with your girlfriend early on in the relationship, so that neither of you feel pressured or uncomfortable with how far things are progressing physically.

14. What are the signs and symptoms of being pregnant?
For most people the first sign that they are pregnant is that they miss a period; this is called amenorrhoea. This is the most important sign, though if your periods are irregular it can be difficult to tell if this is due to pregnancy or just the irregularity.

There are many other symptoms but not everyone gets all of them. Some people get none of them. They may include sore/tender breasts, nausea (that may or may not be worse in the mornings), being more tired than normal and passing urine more frequently. The nausea tends to occur later, usually about seven weeks after your last period.

Discharges, whether in pregnancy or not, can be normal or abnormal. Discharge in pregnancy can be due to normal mucus, bleeding (if brown), leakage of the fluid surrounding the baby (amniotic fluid) or infection. Whether discharge is abnormal or not depends on its colour, smell and amount. You should attend your GP about any unusual discharge. If you suspect that you are pregnant, you should make an appointment with your doctor as early as possible.

15. I'm definitely pregnant, it's been confirmed by the doctor. I'm so scared. What should I do now?
This must be a very difficult and scary time for you finding out you are pregnant. It is important that you now take the time to fully consider your options before making a decision. Both you and the father, along with family and trusted adults, need to talk the situation through rather than making a decision quickly and regretting it later. It may seem impossible to tell your parent or guardian, but often talking to them helps, even though they may be shocked or upset at first. In my experience, parents/guardians are almost always supportive, and if you were to think of the roles being reversed, wouldn't you want to be there for your daughter if she were pregnant?

In your situation, you have three options. You can keep the baby, have the baby adopted or you can have an abortion. (In Northern Ireland abortion is illegal in most instances.) None of these options are easy and all will have major implications on your future. I would like to point out that abortion is sometimes viewed as the easiest way out but unfortunately there is no way of turning the clock back afterwards and abortion can have serious effects both physically and emotionally in years to come.

I would really encourage you to talk through your situation at length and take your time before making your decision. A local crisis pregnancy centre, your own doctor, as well as your parents/guardians, or perhaps a youth leader or pastoral care teacher will be able to offer you advice and support. It certainly would be best if you do not rush the decision, as often it may take a while to come to terms with what has happened, to have more clarity to see the way ahead and to see how each choice could affect your future and the future of your baby.

Chapter 7

Different, But the Same?
Homosexuality and Bisexuality

Mary can't stop wrestling with a heartfelt dilemma after Dean makes his underwater confession to her in the opening sequence of *Saved* (2004).

'How could my boyfriend be gay. He's the best Christian I know? Why has he been stricken with such a spiritually toxic affliction?' she wonders.

The film may be sublimely tongue-in-cheek, but the issues raised are real. The morality of homosexuality is one of the most pressing controversies for Christians today. *Saved*'s Pastor Skipp speaks for many in telling Dean that 'this is not a grey area. There is no room for moral ambiguity. The Bible is black and white.'

Surely he is right? You can't get much clearer than Leviticus 20:13: 'If a man lies with a man as one lies with a woman, both of them have done what is detestable.' However, things may seem less clear when, a few verses on, we read that we can also make ourselves detestable by failing to distinguish between 'clean and unclean animals and between unclean and clean birds' Anyone want to defend this one for Christians today? Still more puzzling: although preachers often attribute the destruction of Sodom to its citizens' homosexuality (Genesis 19), the Bible itself is perfectly clear that it was primarily because they were 'arrogant, overfed and unconcerned' with the poor, that they were destroyed (Ezekiel 16:49).

Even Romans 1, the longest and most detailed reference to homosexual acts in the New Testament, is often misunderstood. The context of the 'shameful' nature referred to (Romans 1:26,27) is actually idolatry, of which homosexual sex is but a powerful example. Paul is concerned here about the spiritual meaning of homosexual sex. One theologian pinpoints this meaning as rejecting the Otherness of God and trying to make 'sameness' divine instead (Henri Blocher, *In the Beginning*, 1984, IVP). God made us male and female to complement each other and to indicate in bodily form our interdependence. Homosexual sex distorts this meaning, no matter how loving and committed the partners may be.

This does not mean, however, that those with homosexual or bisexual feelings are less created in God's image or less loved by him than those who never miss a heartbeat for someone of the same sex all their lives. Heterosexuals, bisexuals and homosexuals, along with drunks, thieves and the just plain greedy were all welcomed into the New Testament church alike, through the common entrance of repentance (1 Corinthians 6:9–11). What then does repentance practically entail for those with homosexual or bisexual orientations?

For Dean in *Saved*, it involves his clueless parents shipping him off to the 'Mercy House' for 'degayification'. However, instead of being 'degayified' he learns that Jesus loves him even though he is homosexually oriented. Whether gay, straight or bisexual, we are all answerable to God for our sexual actions but our sexual (and other) feelings are not automatically temptations, let alone sins. Mary challenges Pastor Skipp over his own feelings towards her mother, 'It's all too much to live up to. No one fits in 100 per cent of the time. Not even you.'

She is right. It is all too much, even with the help of Jesus, *if* he is only a Jesus of our own imagination or culture as in *Saved*. The Jesus of the Gospels, however, is able to help us, whatever our sexual orientation, to 'go and sin no more' but also in our sexual failings, he assures us, 'Neither do I condemn you' (John 8:11, NKJV). As *Saved*'s Mary says to her self-righteous friend, Hilary-Faye, who has just angrily hurled a Bible at her, 'This is not a weapon, you idiot.' With regard to attacking people, she is right again.

Questions and Answers

1. What does homosexual mean? I've heard a lot of people call other people 'homos'.

There are varying definitions of homosexuality but the key thing in my view is a fixed sexual orientation leading to an exclusive desire to have genital sexual acts with others of the same sex as you.

Romantic feelings, and certainly feelings of affection for others of the same sex are not the same as homosexuality and are felt by many heterosexuals, bisexuals and of course homosexuals.

Sexuality is a complex thing and research indicates that among those who self-identify as homosexuals over 90 per cent of both sexes have had sexual partners of the opposite sex too.

Calling people 'homos' is not good. Whether someone is homosexual, bisexual or heterosexual, any form of verbal abuse of anyone on the basis of his or her sexual orientation is totally unacceptable.

2. I am in love, like totally in love, not a crush or a feeling. The only problem is that this person is a girl and she doesn't know I am a lesbian. I need to tell her my feelings soon before my brain explodes with all my feelings for her. I am too shy to tell her and explain to her. (Female, 13)

Can I first reassure you that at 13 it is not uncommon to feel this way about someone of the same sex.

Often as you are growing up you can feel incredibly strong feelings like this and it is OK! Sometimes the feelings can change, at other times your feelings may continue.

Most teenagers identify with a heterosexual attraction by late teens but some still believe their orientation is homosexual by late/mid-teens on and by orientation they could be defined then as having a homosexual identity.

It may be best, therefore, not to talk your feelings through with this other girl. By saying you are a lesbian at 13 you may be putting yourself in a situation where you could be misunderstood and hurt emotionally. Society sometimes likes to label us by our orientation rather than seeing each of us as much more than that. Have you talked to anyone about how you are feeling? Maybe it would be helpful to talk with someone who is older and who you can trust.

Can I encourage you not to speak or act too quickly. Enjoy the friendship of as many girls and boys of your age as you can. Relax. Try not to rush things.

3. I am 14 and I am experiencing attraction to someone of the same sex as me. Does this mean I am gay?

The experience of attraction to someone of the same sex can be a positive foundation for many life-

enhancing friendships or other meaningful relationships which do not need to involve engaging in sex.

Equally, as is the case of having sexual feelings for
the opposite sex, sexual feelings may pass or
diminish with time. Even if they don't, they do not
necessarily have to be acted on, in the same way that
sexual feelings for someone of the opposite sex do
not have to be acted upon.

You are still developing emotionally and psychologically and I would suggest that you take your
time and don't rush things. As in all situations, it can
be useful to have a chat with someone at home or a
teacher in the pastoral care team at school.

**4. My friend and I have been talking about kissing
each other (we are both girls). I don't know how
she really feels, or how I really feel, but I would
like to see what it is like. Would you advise this?
(14)**

From what you are saying, it seems that you are
unsure about your feelings. In all areas, experi-
mentation is not the best way to test your feelings.
By kissing your friend 'sexually' you could cause
confusion to yourself, her or others and it might also
ruin a good friendship. Relax and avoid experimen-
tation. With time you will have a better chance of
understanding your sexual orientation.

5. Is it OK to be homosexual, 'cos I am? I only tried it out to see what it was like but then I found myself attracted to the opposite sex as well.

Having homosexual feelings is not uncommon and it doesn't mean that you are abnormal in any way. Studies show that nearly half of young men have had at least one orgasm stimulated by homosexual thoughts, yet only 1 to 2 per cent of men are exclusively homosexual, some are bisexual and the majority are heterosexual.

An orgasm can be a very powerful experience, however, and repeatedly having them in a homo-sexual context can modify your sexual preferences as well as be a result of them. Trying out gay sex (or indeed straight sex) can often be very unwise when you are in your early teens, as a degree of uncertainty about sexual orientation is common at your age.

It is better to allow normal emotional develop-ment to continue until you are sure about how you really feel. It is only when you are in your late teens and early twenties that you can be fairly sure about the certainty of sexual preferences; and even after that things can sometimes change.

6. Is someone who is homosexual more at risk of specific sexual infections/diseases?

Someone is not at greater risk of specific infections or medical problems simply because they have a

particular sexual orientation, whether that is heterosexual, bisexual or homosexual. Rather a person's
own individual sexual infection/disease risk is
influenced by their own personal sexual behavioural
choices as outlined below:

- Sexually transmitted infections including HIV can
  be passed through any sexual relationship.

- The more sexual partners a person has and the
  more casual they are regarding sex, the greater the
  likelihood of contracting infections.

- Anal sex carries a greater risk of infection than
  vaginal sex, which carries a greater risk than oral
  sex.

- Practising safer sex (*proper* use of condoms *every*
  time) reduces the infection risk. Note that it does
  not completely remove the infection risk.
  Condoms can slip or burst and condoms are also
  more effective with regard to some infections than
  others.

In summary: the risks of picking up sexually
transmitted infections are based on one's sexual
behavioural choices.

7. I have very strong feelings towards a male teacher. Please help? (Male, 15)

Emotions can be very unpredictable things and sexual attraction to teachers can be very strong, whether heterosexual, bisexual or homosexual. This unpredictability means, however, that we can get the 'hots' for someone, only to find that three or four months later the passion has cooled completely. However, even if your feelings last, you may put your teacher's career at risk if you were to get involved sexually with him. Your relationship with him on other levels may also be wrecked.

Research shows that around a quarter of boys of your age are uncertain about their sexual orientation. But by the age of 18 this number has fallen dramatically.

Nonetheless, homosexual feelings, as you say, can be overpowering, especially in Western society which does not encourage the development of even strong non-sexual friendships between men.

You may need to explore your feeling towards your teacher a little more closely. Are they feelings of attraction, admiration, hero-worship or a desire to have sex with him. If they are the latter, it would be very unwise for you to act on them. You are under the legal age of consent and your teacher would be breaking the law, and you would be at risk of getting a sexually transmitted disease even if condoms were used for sex.

8. I have had feelings for other guys for as long as I can remember. Is it possible for me to change? (Male, 16)

I can't tell from your question whether you have only had feelings for guys or whether you have experienced feelings for girls too. Sometimes, as one is developing things can change and sometimes during puberty there can be an uncertainty about sexual orientation. The majority of people would eventually identify as heterosexual, some would identify as bisexual and a smaller number as exclusively homosexual in orientation.

You feel fairly certain that your orientation is exclusively homosexual. Working through such an orientation can be quite a struggle, as can the choices around how you choose to live life regarding sexual behaviour, given the feelings you have.

Regarding possible change in sexual orientation, certainly there are some people who say they have experienced an orientation change; others say it is not possible and they would say that those who claim such change were possibly bisexual in orientation in the first place. The wish to change from a homosexual orientation most often, but not always, arises from a religious conviction.

Ultimately, if an individual chooses to pursue change in any area of their life, that should be respected as a human right as much as their choice to pursue other lifestyle choices. They may find that radical change is or is not possible through counselling, but help in understanding and dealing with their sexual feelings and finding alternative patterns of behaviour if desired, is always available. For some young people, that alternative pattern of behaviour may be not being sexually active and that pattern, if chosen, is a healthy one irrespective of an individual's sexual orientation.

There are many websites widely advertised for those who choose to embrace a homosexual lifestyle. There are other websites available that may be useful to a young person who is unsure of their orientation or who is seeking to review their sexual choices.

Remember that, as with all other areas around relationships and choices, it can be helpful to talk to someone within the pastoral care team at school or your GP, your parent or another trusted adult.

9. Last night, my friend asked me to give him oral sex. I said I didn't know how, so he gave me some. It felt great. Does this mean I am gay?
Just because it felt great, doesn't mean you are gay. The first experience of a new sexual behaviour can be very overwhelming and it means no more than that you found it pleasurable, as sex often is.

Whether it was wise is another matter. Oral sex (especially without using a condom or dental dam) is not a good idea, whether with another male or with a female. Many STIs, especially herpes, are spread by oral sex but more worryingly, life-threatening infections such as HIV and syphilis can be transmitted as well. These last two conditions are much more common in the UK in men who have sex with other men, and oral sex is the main mode of spread for syphilis.

Sex at its best expresses love as well as making you feel great. What your male friend has done to you has put you both at risk. You should encourage him to get an STI test carried out at a GUM clinic as soon as possible and you should do the same.

The emotional impact of this experience should also be considered. You should talk the situation through with a parent or an adult you can trust as you need help to work through what actually happened.

10. I know that I am gay and not bisexual. I don't like girls or women and my boyfriend feels the same way. I can't imagine life without him. We like the same things, laugh at the same jokes and are good at the same sports. How can this be wrong?
It sounds as if you have an incredible friendship. We all need soul mates and most of the things you talk about are things that two intimate friends of the same sex can and should share together no matter what others might think.

When it comes to two males having sex with each other, however, even if they both feel passionately

that this is the only way they will ever find meaningful sexual expression, you do need to be aware that
there are greater dangers than those facing straight
couples.

Anal sex is a high-risk activity, whether with men
or women. Although not all homosexual couples
have anal sex, the rate of anal cancer in men who
have sex with men is now higher than the rate of
cervical cancer in women. Condoms certainly make
sex safer but there are no condoms licensed as safe
for anal sex, though using the strongest types is
obviously safer. The lining of the rectum is much
more delicate than that of the vagina. It tears more
easily and is therefore more prone to dangers of
infection.

Of course, unfaithfulness is sadly all too common
in both heterosexual and homosexual relationships
but the consequences are potentially much more
serious for men having sex with other men as, in the
UK, the majority of cases of HIV and AIDS are still
within the gay community.

Our sexual lives, whether gay, straight or 'grey',
can often be like a rollercoaster. I would encourage
you to talk further with a trusted adult about this
issue, so as to help you explore your feelings more
fully. I hope this information is helpful as you make
your lifestyle choices.

Chapter 8

Making or Faking Love?
Sexual Intercourse

In the film *Vanilla Sky* (2001), Tom Cruise plays handsome publishing tycoon David Aames who, after meeting the glamorous Sofia at a party, spends the night at her apartment. They don't have sex, but when David leaves the next morning, he has a tough time convincing his girlfriend Julie of this when he finds her waiting for him outside in her car, having followed him the previous night.

As Julie drives David away, they have a passionate argument, during which she asks him, 'Don't you know, David, that when you make love to me, your body makes a promise, even if you don't?'

He looks back at her, eyes widening with either sudden understanding or incomprehension. We don't discover which, as she drives off the road, over a bridge and into a wall, killing herself and scarring David for life, so that he has to wear a mask like the Phantom of the Opera thereafter.

Julie's question points to something that those who share their bodies in the mystery of sex often recognize deep down in their hearts – something that the Bible revealed and explained thousands of years ago – that sex is a means of communicating, a giving of the self, the making of a promise. 'Do you not know,' asks Paul of the Corinthian Christians, 'that he who unites himself with a prostitute is one with her in body? For it is said, "The two will become one flesh"' (1 Corinthians 6:16). Corinth was the 'Sin City' of its day and Paul is astonished that in such a sexualized environment, Christians fail to appreciate that sex is a spiritual business. Even what they might consider the most casual of sexual unions, is anything *but* casual. A spiritual bonding takes place in having sex which is irreversible.

So precious, intimate and wonderful is the union of a man and woman in sexual intercourse, that the Bible says it mirrors the union that Christ has with the church, which is his bride (Ephesians 5:31–33). Here, too, the creation principle of the two becoming 'one flesh' (Genesis 2:24) is quoted, as it is by Jesus himself (Matthew 19:4–6) when he affirms both the goodness and God-givenness of sex. But Jesus adds that this God-given sexual union is meant to be permanent and whoever God joins together 'let man not separate' (Matthew 19:6). Separating sexual union from marital union is also something we should not do. God often speaks of his faithful, committed love to his people in sexual terms, e.g. 'I looked at you and saw that you were old enough for love' (Ezekiel 16:8) and ' "In that day," declares the Lord, "you will call me 'my husband'"' (Hosea 2:16). Sex outside of the commitment of marriage violates this aspect of the revealed nature of God's love and causes sex to lose its integrity to a greater or lesser degree.

The choices you make as a teenager will affect the rest of your life. This is why again and again in the answers in this section, we emphasize the importance of saving sex for marriage, as opposed to the usual mantra of 'safe' sex. Sexual mistakes can be forgiven but so often their consequences cannot be undone.

Questions and Answers

1. We both never really plan to go as far as we do (we have never had full sex) but always end up doing stuff we regret, or at least I do. How can I stop this happening?

Your question raises some very important issues involved within intimate relationships between young people. Two things that you will need to consider are: firstly, how far is too far, so as to know where to set appropriate boundaries and secondly, how do we maintain agreed boundaries?

Boundaries are important in all relationships and will be especially important in your relationship with your partner. Agreed boundaries set out both what is OK to do and what isn't. Remember it is much better and easier to have discussed and agreed these before you get carried away in the heat and passion of the moment. Decide to go no further than kissing (above the neck!) because when you start to go further and get sexually aroused, full sexual intercourse can very easily happen. I would encourage you not to get involved in behaviour that consistently builds up sexual arousal, preparing the body for sexual intercourse. Unless you want this to happen, it is an unloving thing to arouse your partner to this extent if you have previously agreed that you will not have intercourse.

You also say, 'at least I do'. Have you discussed with your partner their feelings about where things are currently going physically in the relationship and whether they are comfortable or uncomfortable. You need to express your discomfort and establish your own boundaries, whether or not your partner is agreeable. If they do not respect your boundaries, then I would question their respect and indeed their love for you.

You must take control of what you want to happen and never feel pressured to do something you don't want to. Set boundaries and stick to them.

2. I have been going out with my girlfriend for a few months now. We have decided not to have sex but are happy to do other stuff. I was wondering are there still any risks involved, even if you don't actually have sex?

A good place to start answering your question is by exploring what 'other stuff' might involve. This might mean anything from holding hands to genital contact. There is quite a range of activities, all involving different levels of arousal. Whilst holding hands can provoke intense sexual arousal, it is less likely to do so than touching your partner's genital areas. When you start to touch parts of the other person that you don't have, then you are generally into sexual foreplay (activities which a couple do when planning to have sex).

When you are involved in sexual foreplay, the chance of you having full sex is increased, as it can be very difficult in the heat of the moment to stop going further than you had planned. Remember, too, that oral sex is also sexual intercourse and sexually transmitted infections including gonorrhoea and herpes simplex are all commonly transmitted by oral sex. In fact, these infections can be passed by contact with the genital skin of someone else who is infected.

I am concerned for you, because if you are regularly involved in sexual foreplay with your girlfriend at present, it may not be long before you progress to vaginal sex and at a young age, this level of sexual involvement is too intense to be adequately supported by the level of commitment in the rest of your relationship. I would advise you to cool things down, take time to talk about your relationship, and spend more of your time together finding out about each other, free from the pressures and risks associated with sexual foreplay or sexual inter-course.

3. What is mutual masturbation?
Mutual masturbation is a very intimate sexual act in which each partner stimulates the other to orgasm without penetration. It can, however, often lead on to full penetrative intercourse within a very short period of time, whether it was intended to happen or not. You should ask yourself if you are ready for this and what the consequences of this type of

activity might be for you. It is important to realize that sexual touching is intended to be an expression of the depth of loving commitment between two lovers and when such touching is used in a selfish way just to gain personal satisfaction or release, there is always an eventual price to pay. Feeling guilty, used, empty, angry, addicted to sexual stimulation or deeply cynical about loving relationships can all result, among other things.

Talk about your feelings and what you want. Don't rush the physical side of your relationship, as love is more than feelings and more than sex.

4. Do you have to have oral sex or other forms of sexual foreplay first, before you have full sex?

No, you do not have to have oral sex before having vaginal intercourse. Many married couples who have been sexual partners for decades may never have oral sex. Oral sex involves using the mouth to stimulate the sexual organs of your partner. Cunnilingus (slang 'licking out') is the term used when oral sex is performed on a female and fellatio (slang 'blow job') is the term used when oral sex is performed on a male. Oral sex can transmit a number of STIs.

Sexual intercourse can occur without foreplay taking place. However, in practice foreplay often does precede sexual intercourse, as it has the purpose of stimulating the sexual organs so as to be well lubricated in preparation for penetrative sex.

If you have not already had sex, please consider delaying having intercourse, at least until you would be ready to cope with the negative consequences that may result: pregnancy, STIs and the emotional hurt which is often associated.

Remember, if your boyfriend/girlfriend really loves you they will respect you and respect your decisions. Don't be afraid to wait: most other younger teenagers are still virgins; you are included within the majority!

I would also remind you that you do not have to make the same decisions in the future as you may have made in the past. Assess your lifestyle choices, be informed and make the best choices for you and your health – physically, emotionally, psychologically and spiritually.

5. My mate said you could get an STI from kissing, is this true?

The answer to your question depends largely on what sort of kissing is involved and what is being kissed.

A normal kiss on the lips is absolutely safe and you would have nothing to worry about with regard to STIs (though cold sores can be caught). However, if the kissing gets a bit more intense and passionate and develops to the extent that it involves kissing or stimulating with your mouth the genital area of your partner, then risks of STIs are present.

Such kissing (oral sex) can spread cold sores that appear on your mouth to the genital areas. This is called genital herpes simplex infection. It can be very painful and recurrent so if either of you have cold sores or have had them at any time then there is some risk.

So your mate was right to some extent in what they said, but rest assured that normal kissing on the lips is perfectly safe and definitely enjoyable!

6. What is an orgasm?

An orgasm (a climax or 'coming') is the intense wave of sexual excitement or pleasure in response to sexual stimulation that can be experienced by both men and women.

In men an orgasm is accompanied by the ejaculation of semen from the penis. In women, there is no such clearly defined objective way of knowing an orgasm has occurred, only the individual experience, which is difficult to define in words but unmistakable once felt!

Some young people wonder whether orgasm is harmful in any way. It is not, and it won't do any damage to either the man's or woman's body.

Where sexual foreplay and sexual intercourse are enjoyed in a committed lifelong relationship – the best example of which is marriage – both parties can learn how to bring most pleasure to each other and this can compliment all other areas of their relationship/friendship. Outside of this sort of relationship, and especially among young people, there are many risks involved in activity that leads to orgasm – activity I would encourage you to delay until you are committed to one person for life.

7. My boyfriend and I had 'dry sex'. We both had our underwear on. I'm not sure if he came but I'm scared some of his pre-cum maybe soaked through my underwear. I am so scared. Could I be pregnant?
Pre-ejaculatory fluid ('pre-cum') is produced during sexual arousal as a natural lubricant to facilitate sexual intercourse occurring. Sperm are often present in pre-ejaculatory fluid. 'Dry sex' can, as you have experienced, turn out to be rather more moist than couples expect!

You should certainly get a pregnancy test done if your period is late, though the risk of being pregnant is probably low.

In the heat of the moment, there is a high risk, however, of such intimate sexual activity progressing on to full penetrative sex. It sounds as if you should discuss with your boyfriend where your relationship is going and where you actually want it to go.

You may well have to review your choices together and put boundaries in place to prevent things becoming even more sexual and your fears about pregnancy becoming a reality.

8. When my girlfriend and I get together we both feel really horny and turned on. Do you think it is better that she pulls me off rather than having full sex?

Whether your girlfriend 'pulls you off' (masturbates you to orgasm) or you have penetrative sex, both are a major deal and this is something that first and foremost you need to discuss with your girlfriend. It is common for mutual masturbation to lead to full vaginal intercourse and I wonder whether you are both ready for the potential consequences of this. It is very important within a relationship that both partners feel comfortable and are happy with how things are developing – especially when it comes to sex.

You should chat in advance about how far you are both happy to take things, discussing and agreeing boundaries of what is OK and what's not. It is important to remember that neither you nor your girlfriend should feel pressured into doing anything you are not comfortable with. If your girlfriend does not want to do things you would like her to do, if you love her, you will respect her wishes and support her in her decision.

Making the choice to refrain from intimate sexual contact in a relationship is a good choice. It means you don't have to worry about becoming a father, or picking up an STI, and imagine how much more hurt you would be if you and your girlfriend had sex and then broke up, compared to if you hadn't had sex. Instead of worrying about the physical side of your relationship and all the consequences of it, you will be free to get to know each other better, spending time chatting together, going out as a couple with other friends – all of which will develop your friendship and enable you to find out whether there is a future in the two of you being together.

Sex is a special thing, not something to be taken casually. It should be respected and, ideally, you should wait till you are sure you have found your lifelong partner who you can commit to in marriage.

9. What age do you have to be to have sex?

This is a very important question, and to answer it I shall concentrate on two key aspects.

Firstly, the law in Scotland, England and Wales states that you have to be 16 before you can legally have sex (often called 'the age of consent'). In Northern Ireland, you have to be 17. This law is there to protect you, not to spoil your fun. Evidence clearly shows that the younger someone starts having sex (especially when under the legal age), the more likely it is that they may suffer from unpleasant physical and emotional consequences.

Secondly, apart from the law, you should fully consider the reasons you want to have sex and the responsibilities and consequences involved in having sexual intercourse. Perhaps a good question to ask is: At what age would you be ready to have a baby or to deal with the emotional effects of sharing your body so intimately with someone else, or to risk picking up an STI?

There is more and more pressure on young people today to experiment with sex to gain experience to see if they are compatible with their partner. This is a very misleading concept, however, as incompatibility is rarely if ever a sexual issue but rather usually relates to personality and emotion. I would recommend that you spend time with your friends, possibly on group dates, getting to know members of the 'opposite sex' better, but leaving the intimate physical side of the relationship until you are sure that the person you have found is the person you wish to spend the rest of your life with.

10. Does it hurt the first time you have sex?
Sex may hurt the first time for a girl, especially if she feels pressured or if there is no tenderness or a context in which she can feel secure. There may be a little pain and/or loss of blood when the hymen (a piece of tissue over the vaginal opening) is torn. This may already be broken for example if tampons have previously been used.

Like any form of physical contact, discomfort or pain also depends on how vigorously it is carried out. If it is physically painful, this may be the result of not being relaxed or having a partner who is more interested in satisfying themselves than expressing love to the other person. There is also the emotional pain if the circumstances are not right or if a person is worried about the consequences of having sex. Less often, a medical problem can cause recurrent pain during sex.

Sex at its best is a wonderful thing when shared between two people who are fully committed to each other. Having sex for the first time should be a wonderful experience with someone fully committed to you, who you can trust and who has your best interests at heart. In this situation you are most likely to be treated with the respect, gentleness and love you deserve.

11. I feel ready to have sex. My boyfriend and I have talked it through and are sure it is what we both want. How can we be sure to avoid pregnancy and STIs?

Thanks for your question, which shows your consideration for your boyfriend and maturity in not just rushing headlong into sex. It is worth considering that by having sex at a younger age there are some risks that you will expose yourself to which are reduced by waiting. For example, girls who have first intercourse aged 14 or less have twice the risk of developing cancer of the cervix than those who wait until they are over 18. There is no evidence that condoms reduce this excess risk.

Condoms are often said to be adequate protection against pregnancy and STIs, but this is not so. The failure rate of condoms is around 15 per cent among teenagers. This means that on average they will fail one in every seven times they are used. Sex with a condom may be safer than sex without, but it is not safe sex. Most doctors would advise that, if you are having sex, the most effective protection you can have is to use a condom every time to give as much protection against STIs as you can *and* to go onto the combined contraceptive pill which offers the best protection against pregnancy (but none against STIs). It is important to remember, though, that you will have to use condoms correctly each and every time you have sex and will have to take the pill every day. Few teenagers manage to achieve this and there is considerable evidence that inconsistent use of condoms is associated with an increased risk of getting an STI.

Having covered the medical information, it is worth considering some other aspects and options. When sex enters a teenage relationship, quite often it has the opposite effect than expected and the relationship fizzles out and ends. If you truly love each other, isn't waiting until you are absolutely sure you are committed to each other lifelong the best thing?

It is often helpful to talk through such an important decision such as 'starting to have sex' with a parent or another adult who knows you well. They can sometimes offer a more objective perspective than you, when you are in love and can never imagine that your relationship will end.

The surest way to avoid both pregnancy and sexually transmitted infection is not to have sex with anyone until you are sure that your love for them is so committed that you will have sex with them and only them for the rest of your lives. Are you both ready for this? If not, then sex is unwise, no matter what friends or society might suggest.

12. My girlfriend wants me to have sex with her but because of my religious views I don't think I should. What should I do?
Your question is a good one as you are obviously thinking through the choices you face and your own personal values and beliefs.

All choices that people make can either be consistent with or contradict their own moral or ethical code. Often when we choose to do things that are not consistent with our background or personal beliefs, we feel guilty. Often, though, when we choose and behave in a way that is consistent with our own personal values we are more comfortable and contented with the choices we have made.

Has your girlfriend communicated to you her desire to have sex or do you just assume she may want sex? It would be good to tell her what you want out of the relationship. If appropriate, you may want to approach her and tell her that you really like her, but you're not prepared to have sex.

Communicate why you think sex is not appropriate from your religious perspective and then draw the line where you feel is the safest place for you physically.

Most likely, she will respect your decision to say 'no' to sex, but if she is offended, she may not be best for you. Her response might dictate the next steps you should make – whether to stay with her or not.

13. How do you actually have sex?
Vaginal sexual intercourse (coitus or copulation) involves the insertion of the erect penis of the male into the vagina of the female. Having sex is usually preceded by sexual foreplay, which leads to sexual arousal of the partners, resulting in erection of the penis and natural lubrication of the vagina. The erect penis is inserted into the vagina and one or both of the partners move back and forth to stimulate themselves and each other, usually to the point of ejaculation and orgasm.

Sex is more, though, than just merely a physical act for your own or indeed your partner's pleasure. Sex is designed to make babies and as an emotional, and indeed spiritual experience that should be an expression of true love designed to connect and unite two people.

Sex may involve a whole range of emotions such as love, trust, joy, pleasure, fear, regret, guilt, excitement, pain and relief. Sex is more than just a simple physical recreational activity. It is relational, involving two people in a most intimate and special way sharing each other's bodies: the pleasure of one another stemming from this intimacy.

14. My boyfriend and I have decided not to have sex but find it very difficult when people make fun of our decision. All my friends seem to be having sex. How can I be sure we have made the right decision?
I think it is great that you and your boyfriend are able to talk through such an important decision as this, whether or not to have sex, and that you have decided to wait. Let me reassure you that not having sex at your age means you are part of the majority and not the minority. Research confirms that the vast majority of boys and girls of your age have not had sex (around 70 per cent of under 16-year-olds have not had sex) and those who do experience sex early usually regret it.

Quite often, those who brag the most about their sexual experiences are those who are doing the least – so don't be fooled by big talk.

Let me encourage you to continue to wait until you both feel you are ready to commit to each other for the rest of your life. It is worth remembering that you may break up with your current boyfriend (even if at the moment this seems impossible), and you may have other boyfriends before you finally settle down. How much worse would the break up be if sex had been part of the relationship? And, if sex were to be part of any future relationships, how much more difficult would those break-ups be and what effect would they have on your future relationship with your future husband? Do you want to have had sex with other men and be in the position of having to tell your husband about them? Or would you rather be free from the worry of comparison, STIs and emotional hurt?

Be proud of the decision you have made. You are a positive example to your friends and rather than them influence you, you are in a great position to show to them how great a relationship can be without sex being an essential part of it. You are making the best decision for you and your boyfriend and for your future husband and indeed your boyfriend's future wife, whoever they may be!

15. I'm thinking about having sex with my boyfriend but wondering if I should. I'm afraid he won't like my body and that I won't match up to his previous girlfriends. What should I do?
Basically, the question you are asking is, are you ready for sex? I suppose the simple answer is that if you view sex as only a physical thing, then any adolescent would be ready. But it is much more than just the physical, isn't it?

Just think a while before you act. What if your boyfriend and you have sex, then it doesn't work out? How hurtful will it be to see him going out with someone else, knowing that you were physically and emotionally bonded in such a special way with him?

Even now, you seem to have some reservations because you think you won't match up to his past girlfriends. And if you are feeling uncomfortable about him seeing your body, I wonder whether he is showing you the respect and love that you deserve, which should be part of any long-lasting relationship.

If he has had previous sexual partners, then having sex with him would put you at risk of STIs and he may well be carrying infections from previous partners without even being aware that he has them.

If you think this is the guy for you, then I'd advise you to make sure he wants you just as you are – a unique and very special person. If he just wants sex, and you don't give it, he'll fast move on to someone else. Is this the type of guy you want?

If he is willing to wait for sex because he thinks you are special enough to wait for, then he is showing strength of character and may be more the type of guy you deserve to be with. You deserve the best – don't settle for anything less.

16. I got drunk at a party and think I had sex, but I'm not really sure. One of the boys the next day said he had slept with me. What should I do?

Thanks for the question. Firstly, just because this guy is saying that he had sex with you, doesn't mean that he did. Sometimes, in order to be 'one of the lads', guys will exaggerate or make up stories about sex and who they had sex with.

How well do you know this guy? Have you spoken to him since? Do you feel you could talk to him? Perhaps if you talked to him face-to-face he may have a different story!

If you were extremely drunk, it can be difficult to know. If, on reflection or after talking to the guy, you feel you may have had sex or if you are still uncertain, it would be important to visit your GP or a local crisis pregnancy centre if your period does not come, to get a pregnancy test done. You can buy test kits in a pharmacy and do one yourself. A positive result should always be confirmed. You would also need to get checked out for STIs, even if you had intimate physical contact without full sex. Viral STIs such as herpes and HPV can be passed on without full sex taking place.

I would imagine this incident has made you think about what can happen when you drink alcohol, and in this case getting really drunk. Alcohol can make you do things that perhaps you wouldn't normally do and can leave you in such a position that others may be able to take advantage of you. I would encourage you to avoid alcohol and by doing so you will avoid something like this happening again.

At times like this it is always good to talk to someone you can trust, like an older friend, parent, guardian or teacher for advice and support. It may be difficult and a bit embarrassing but people with your best interests at heart, usually have the best advice and opportunity to help.

17. When is a girl at her most fertile and when would be the best time to have sex with my girlfriend if I don't want to make her pregnant?
To get straight to the point and dispel the myth, pregnancy can occur at any time of the month. Yes, even during your girlfriend's period!

This means you can never be absolutely sure that sex, at anytime, will not lead to pregnancy. In theory, the first few days after your girlfriend's period and the last few before her period are the times when she is least likely to get pregnant.

Adults in committed relationships can improve on just guesswork by the woman monitoring her temperature or the consistency of her cervical mucus for a few months so that she can predict her most fertile time. This can be a useful method of contraception but works best among committed couples that have been and plan to continue to be together long term.

Pregnancy can happen very easily; contraception

makes it less likely, but it doesn't totally eradicate the possibility. So if you aren't ready for a baby, I would suggest you aren't truly ready for sex.

18. I have been going with my boyfriend for just over three months and recently he has asked me to have sex with him. I have told him I'm not ready but he keeps bringing the topic up again and says things like 'he only wants to have sex if I'm ready and that it's my choice'. What is the best way for me to tell him I don't want to have sex? I need him to understand what I want and to stop putting me under pressure.

This is a very common situation faced by many girls, and indeed boys may face similar pressures from their girlfriends. I would encourage you by saying that your question shows you have a very mature attitude to this important area of your relationship.

I would be concerned, as your boyfriend is keen to have sex with you, despite you telling him you are not ready. He is applying subtle pressure on you by bringing up the subject so often. I would suggest that you have a good talk with him and explain exactly how you feel. I would tell him that as sex is such a special and beautiful thing, you want to save it for that special person with whom you will spend the rest of your life. This may well be your current boyfriend, however I would have some doubt where the boy does not seem to be prepared to wait or continues to apply pressure, however subtle, when the girl has made it clear that she is not ready. Sometimes it is worth talking the situation through with a parent or another trusted adult so that you are not so isolated in the relationship.

It is great to be in a relationship where two people genuinely care for each other and do not put pressure on each other and instead just enjoy having fun together and really getting to know each other. Many teenagers of your age are still virgins, although the media would tend to give a different message, and this may well have influenced your boyfriend.

If you speak to your boyfriend and tell him exactly how you feel and he respects your decision and applies no further pressure, then I believe that this relationship could be a long-lasting one. However, if he doesn't respect your decision or threatens to break up the relationship if you won't have sex, this would indicate he does not truly respect or love you – and you deserve better. It may be hard, but if that is the case you might have to make the painful decision to end the relationship. That's not easy, but in the long term you deserve the best and you shouldn't settle for less.

Once again, I commend you for your very mature stand and wish you every success in the future.

19. I have been going out with my girlfriend, who is 15, for four months now. We started having sex after three weeks. Do you feel this was too soon to start? I kind of regret it now but I do love her. (Male, 15)

The emotions you are experiencing are very common and indeed quite expected. It is very easy to 'jump' into early sexual relations long before the relationship has properly matured. It is always wise to think of having sex in two main ways. Firstly, one purpose of having sex is to make babies. Are you and your girlfriend prepared to have children now? Secondly, it can be helpful to think of sexual relationships in terms of 'making love'. I would suspect that perhaps to be in love, truly in love and not just having those warm bubbly feelings you experience inside, you certainly need to wait longer than three weeks and I would suggest that you wait even longer than four months.

It is also worth considering your future plans for education, work, travel and how the potential unwanted effects of sexual activity might affect them. Also, having sex with a girl under the age of 16 (17 in Northern Ireland) is illegal and therefore you are actually committing a criminal offence and, though in practice unlikely, the police could get involved if she were to make a complaint about you.

Perhaps you are wisely feeling uncertain about continuing to have sex at present and I would suggest that stopping is a good move that would test how strong your relationship really is. Cooling things down for a while and spending some time apart would be a good idea to help you clarify and sort things out. If you are meant to be together, you will find it hard to be apart for too long. On the other hand, if you enjoy the freedom to do other things with different friends or have other girlfriends, then perhaps things weren't meant to be after all.

Having sex too soon in a relationship can alter the feelings involved: you see each other more in terms of sexual fulfilment, rather than building on each other's personalities and strengths.

Talk to your girlfriend, talk to trusted friends your age and to older people you know as you work this out for yourself. At such a young age, I would strongly recommend you decide not to continue to have sex. Rather you should wait until you are much older and free from all the unnecessary worries that sex brings outside of a committed lifelong relationship such as marriage.

Dictionary of Terms

ABSTINENCE
Refraining from sexual intercourse, whether vaginal, oral or anal. The process of remaining a virgin.

AGE OF CONSENT
The age below which sexual intercourse is against the law and is therefore a criminal offence for the male partner.

AIDS
Acquired Immune Deficiency Syndrome. The final stage of infection with HIV.

BISEXUALITY
Sexual orientation towards people of the same and of the opposite sex.

CERVICAL CANCER
Malignant tumour of the neck of the womb.

CERVIAL SMEAR
A test to pick up early changes of cancer of the neck of the womb (cervix).

CHLAMYDIA
The commonest STI in the UK.

COC
The Combined Oral Contraceptive Pill which contains two hormones, an oestrogen and progestogen.

CONTRACEPTION
Means to avoid or minimise the likelihood of pregnancy resulting from sexual intercourse.

EJACULATION
Release of seminal fluid (semen) from the penis during orgasm.

ERECTION
Hardening and enlargement of the penis from sexual or physical stimulation. Slang terms include 'hard-on' and 'boner'.

FERTILISATION
The process of fusion of egg cell and sperm to form the zygote, the fused cell, which becomes the embryo.

FOREPLAY
Intimate sexual stimulation in preparation for sexual intercourse.

GENITAL
A sexual organ or something related to it.

GLANS
The tip or head of the penis.

GONORRHOEA
A bacterial STI.

GP
General Practitioner or family doctor. The equivalent in the US is a family physician.

GUM CLINC
Genito-Urinary Medicine Clinic, the hospital

141

department which diagnoses and treats sexually transmitted infections. Sometimes known as Special Clinics or STD clinics.

HEPATITIS B
A severe viral infection of the liver, often sexually transmitted.

HERPES
Abbreviation of Herpes Simplex Infection (HSV), a common viral STI.

HETEROSEXUALITY
Sexual orientation towards someone of the opposite sex.

HIV
Human Immunodeficiency Virus, the causal agent of AIDS and. It is often (but not always) sexually transmitted.

HOMOSEXUALITY
Sexual orientation towards someone of the same sex.

HSV
Herpes Simplex Virus.

HPV
Human papillomavirus. The commonest viral STI in the UK. It causes genital warts and is the main cause of cervical cancer.

IMPLANTATION
The embedding of the fertilized egg into the lining of the uterus.

IUD
Intra-Uterine Device. Usually referred to as the 'coil'. A method of contraception.

LYMPH NODE
Glands forming part of the immune system located all over the body and which can enlarge in infections including STIs.

MAP
Morning After Pill, a way of minimising the likelihood of pregnancy occurring which is taken after intercourse. Also known as the 'emergency pill'.

MASTURBATION
Solo sex. Self-stimulation of the genitals to achieve orgasm. Slang terms include 'wanking' and 'tossing off'.

MUTUAL MASTURBATION
Manual stimulation of each other's genitals.

ORGASM
The climax of sexual intercourse comprising of waves of intense pleasure and usually accompanied by ejaculation in the male. Other Slang terms include 'coming' and 'climaxing'and cum.

PENETRATION
Insertion of the penis into the body, either anally, orally or vaginally.

PERIOD
Short for menstrual period, the cyclical (usually) monthly bleed during which the lining of the womb is shed.

PESSARY
A medicine (or medical appliance) for insertion into the vagina.

PID
Pelvic inflammatory disease. Severe infection of the fallopian tubes and pelvic organs often leading to infertility.

POP
Progestogen Only Pill, also known as the 'mini-pill'.

PORNOGRAPHY
Visual or written material produced with the sole or primary aim of sexual arousal during masturbation.

PUBERTY
Phase of growth from child to adult when hormones trigger the development of reproductive function and other sexual characteristics such as under-arm and pubic hair.

PUBES
Slang term for pubic hair.

PUBIC HAIR
Hair around the genital area. Often known as 'pubes'.

SAC
Slang term for scrotum.

SCABIES
A parasitic infection of the pubic hair often transmitted sexually.

SCROTUM
Sac of skin and thin muscles containing the testes. Often known as 'sac'.

SMEAR
Abbreviation of cervical smear, a test to pick up early changes of cancer of the neck of the womb (cervix).

SPHINCTER
Circular ring of muscle often acting as a valve at the entrance or exit of a bodily organ.

STD
Sexually Transmitted Disease (usual term in the USA).

STI
Sexually Transmitted Infection (usual term in the UK).

SYPHILIS
A rapidly increasing STI in the UK and USA.

TRICHOMONAS
A common STI.

VIRGIN
A person who has not had sexual intercourse, whether oral, vaginal or anal.

VULVA
The external sexual parts of a female.

Useful Contacts and Recommended Resources

There are many useful resources available through standard health and educational channels. We have listed just a few that might be of use to a reader interested in a 'Christian perspective':

Websites

Love for Life is a project that supports young people and their carers in the area of relationships and sexuality education.
www.loveforlife.org.uk

True Freedom Trust seeks to support men and women who face same-sex attraction and want to live a life that is in line with biblical teaching.
www.truefreedomtrust.co.uk

The *Becoming Real* website provides help to Christian youth who are confused, questioning or same-sex attracted.
www.becomingreal.org

CAREconfidential offers free, confidential advice if facing an unplanned pregnancy or dealing with post-abortion concerns.
www.careconfidential.com

The *Society of Sexual Health Advisers* is not a Christian organisation but has a list of GUM clinics in the UK, listed by region.
www.ssha.info/public/clinics/locations.asp

Books

Pure Excitement by Joe White (2005, Focus on the Family Publishing) helps teens figure out God's plan for true love and, for those who've made mistakes in the past, walks through the steps to reclaiming purity.

Sex Matters by Steve Chalke and Nick Page (1996, Hodder & Stoughton) explores relationships, sex, love and marriage.

Pure by Linda Marshall (2005, Inter-Varsity Press) explains God's truth and his standard regarding sex and how, with God's grace, young people can stay pure.

Searching for Intimacy by Lyndon Bowring (2005, Authentic Media) offers advice to help people escape from the dangerous web of Internet pornography.

Every Young Man's Battle by Stephen Arterburn and Fred Stoeker (2002, WaterBrook Press) outlines strategies for victory in the real world of sexual temptation.

Every Young Woman's Battle by Shannon Ethridge and Stephen Arterburn (2004, WaterBrook Press) explains how to guard your mind, heart and body in a sex-saturated world.

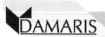

Love for Life

informing choice

Love for Life hope you have found this book of questions and answers helpful. If you have any questions as a result of reading this book or indeed your particular question has not been answered, please be encouraged to email a question to Love for Life through our www.icebergsandbabies.org.uk website.

Love for Life is a project that supports young people and their carers in the area of relationships and sexuality education. We seek to empower young people through supporting their personal development and by helping parents communicate better with their children about sex.

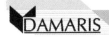

Join Damaris and receive

Discounts on other products from Damaris Books and Damaris Publishing.

Access to Web pages containing up-to-date information about popular culture.

To find out about free membership of Damaris go to www.damaris.org

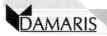
Teenagers
Why Do They Do That?
by Nick Pollard

Concerned about teen drug-taking, pregnancies and eating disorders? Baffled about what drives many teenagers to such behaviour? Worried that 'it must be my fault'?

This brilliantly enlightening book argues that understanding the culture in which teenagers are growing up is the key to understanding why some inflict tragedy upon themselves or others.

Nick Pollard, a specialist in teenage spiritual and moral education, provides adults with invaluable insights to enable them to open doors of communication with teenagers and begin to influence them for good.

DAMARIS

Other Titles from Damaris Books

CultureWatch
(free access website)

CultureWatch explores the message behind the media through hundreds of articles and study guides on films, books, music and television. It is written from a distinctively Christian angle, but is appropriate for people of all faiths and people of no faith at all.

CULTUREWATCH

http://www.damaris.org/cw